ARE THESE YOUR CHILDEN?

Meet Skinny, who said: "I gotta live like a junkie." A year later he was dead.

Meet Jim: Fifteen-year-old son of a district attorney. He's in prison for selling narcotics.

Meet Lawrence: He took LSD and thought he could fly out a sixth-story window. Conclusion: DOA.

David Wilkerson has an answer—the only answer—to youth's desperate and catastrophe-filled search. The answer speaks loudly to the parents of today's teenagers and to much of the falseness of today's adult generation.

Most of all, it speaks loud and clear to youth who stand, lonely, tempted and often without conviction, at the crossroads of decision.

1946

HEY, PREACH . . .
YOU'RE COMIN'
THROUGH!

David Wilkerson

PYRAMID BOOKS *NEW YORK*

Certain names and related details in this book have been altered to protect the identity of those concerned, but to the best of the author's knowledge the facts are absolutely accurate.

HEY, PREACH . . . YOU'RE COMIN' THROUGH!

A PYRAMID BOOK
Published by arrangement with Fleming H. Revell Company

Sixth printing February, 1974

ISBN: 0-515-02419-8

Library of Congress Catalogue Card Number: 68-17096

Printed in the United States of America

Pyramid Books are published by Pyramid Communications, Inc. Its trademarks, consisting of the word "Pyramid" and the portrayal of a pyramid, are registered in the United States Patent Office.

PYRAMID COMMUNICATIONS, INC.
919 Third Avenue, New York, N.Y. 10022, U.S.A.

Contents

Foreword

One of the most exasperating experiences of my life took place last fall, in a church in Finland overflowing with restless young people. The formal liturgy just wasn't reaching them. I was sitting in the ornate chancel, and while the great organ boomed out a stately chorale, I caught the flicker of matches; two bearded youths and a mini-skirted long-haired girl were lighting cigarettes. During a long hymn, I caught the glance exchanged between a wildly dressed girl and her long-haired boy friend in the second pew. It said more eloquently than words, "All this wailing is too much—let's blow!"

That did it. I sent this message to the pastor: "Unless you hand me this meeting in the next two minutes, *I'm leaving!*"

The brutality of those words must have shocked the good minister nearly out of his robes, but he graciously brought the hymn to an abrupt end and welcomed me into the pulpit. What I said there probably shocked him even more. But I wanted to get the attention of those young people *fast*.

That afternoon, as I had walked through the streets of that great Finnish city, I had seen unspeakably

suggestive magazines on display. I had talked with
dozens of confused teen-agers. I had prayed with two
of the most desperate drug addicts in Europe. Now,
as I stood in the pulpit looking out at that great
crowd of young people, I could sense how desperately
many of them were searching for reality. I tried, very
simply and directly, to make clear to them that the
only way out of confusion and boredom is through
complete surrender to Jesus Christ. I told them of the
Power that I personally have seen change the lives of
hundreds of criminals, drug pushers and would-be
suicides.

Before I had finished speaking, I could sense that
that Power was at work in our midst. Slowly, a few at
a time, numbers of those young people began to come
to the front of the great sanctuary and kneel at the
altar. That night more than two hundred of them
crowded forward to find Reality. The sight took me
back to another group of young people—on the side-
walks of New York.

Those New York youngsters had been crowding all
around my street-corner pulpit in one of the city's
worst neighborhoods, but I realized that I wasn't getting through to them. A girl in a tight blouse and skirt
blew cigarette smoke into my face. Boys in bright
shirts pushed against each other. Between whiffs of
tobacco I could smell a sour mixture of bus fumes,
stale perspiration and beer. I tried in vain to lift my
voice above the jeers and curses that slipped so easily
out of those hard young mouths.

I knew that I was on the home "turf" of some of
New York's deadliest gangs; these boys would kill if
the whim struck them. I wasn't afraid of getting

killed, but I *was* afraid of making no impression on these young lives. As the hubbub grew worse, I flashed a desperate prayer to God. I knew that He had brought me to this street corner, and that only He could reach these young people.

Then it happened. A little circle of silence began to widen around me. One pair of eyes after another locked with mine. As I talked of the tremendous Love that could reach out to even the most hardened and unloveable, several teen-agers nodded. Here and there I saw something that might be tears. I knew that God was making contact.

When I had finished, I was surrounded by the leaders of one of the gangs that had terrorized this section of the city. One of them shook his head incredulously, unable to figure out why he was reacting as he did to my simple message. He grabbed my arm and blurted: "*Hey, Preach—you're comin' through!*"

I have been working with young people for ten years now, and in all of them—the students in the average high school or college, the hippies of Haight-Ashbury and the Flower People of Europe—I have sensed the same thing: an intense desire for something genuine and real. Young people today want something to live for, something to believe in, and in their expressions I often read the same message I saw in the face of that New York gang leader years ago:

Mister, you're getting through to me. Man, it's never been like this before—you hit me deep.

In this book I am going to talk as straight and clear as I know how about the problems and possibilities of today's generation, the "now" generation. I want all of you who read this book to get hit hard and deep—so deep you never get over it.

1

The Next Revolution

I will never forget a rally our Teen Challenge workers had on 101st Street in Harlem. About two hundred people gathered near a school building with a good many broken windows, and in the crowd I recognized a number of drug addicts and prostitutes. While my brother Don was leading the singing of "What the World Needs Is Jesus," I went across the street to get a better view of those present.

A well-dressed young social worker I had often seen in the neighborhood came up the street. "Mister," she said, "you're with those hallelujah people over there, aren't you?"

"Yes, I am," I said.

She looked at me suspiciously. "Will you tell me," she asked, "just what you're doing for these people?"

"We're telling them about the Saviour this neighborhood needs."

"I know what you *tell* them," the social worker said. "Christ is the answer! Jesus can change your life! What good does that do a pregnant teen-ager or a hopeless alcoholic? I'm from the welfare department. There isn't much I can do for some of these people, but at least I can see that the hungry children get some food. I can try to get the mothers with rotting teeth to the dentist, and the sick people to the hospital. What most of them need is better housing, more money and a change of environment. Yet you and your hallelujah friends stand there saying that if they surrender to Jesus all their problems are solved. I think it's disgraceful! You say Christ is the answer—but you don't even understand the question!"

She walked away, and I stood there feeling so discouraged that I wondered why I had come to New York. "Lord," I asked, "what *are* we doing here? How can we make a dent in these slums?"

I went back to the rally. While three Bible school trumpeters were playing a gospel medley a dark-haired girl named Rosa slipped to my side and asked softly, "Mr. Wilkerson, was that not the welfare lady who was talking to you just now?"

I nodded, wondering if Rosa had heard her give her opinion of our work.

"You look sad. Did she tell you that our need is money and jobs instead of religion?"

"Yes," I said, "and I'm beginning to wonder if she isn't right. After all, we don't have either money or jobs to offer you people; we had to pray in the money for supper at our own Center the night before last. About all we can offer anyone is faith and prayer."

Rosa looked at me intently. "Mr. Wilkerson, two weeks ago you came to this block with the trumpets and the singing. I came to look, though I laughed when I heard you say that Jesus can live in my heart. That I could not swallow!

"One of your ladies gave me a little black book. She asked me to read it. I laughed at her, too, when she said Jesus would give me power over sin. But that night I started to read this little book that says on the cover, *San Juan*. I like this name, 'John.' I read two chapters. I read how Jesus made water into wine, and I asked Him if He could change my heart.

"Mr. Wilkerson, something happened that night. Ever since, this block has been different. The piles of garbage still smell just as bad, the roaches in our apartment are just as thick, but in some way everything has changed. I have something inside me now that tells me God is with me, and He will be with me anywhere. I have many problems, but Jesus has changed the biggest problem of all. He has shown me how to live with myself."

Rosa smiled. "Mr. Wilkerson, please keep doing what you are doing. Come back often."

I think of Rosa when I see the changes tumbling over each other in the modern world. For a number of years United States crime has been steadily increasing. A year ago that increase doubled. Last summer cities all over America burst into flames. Since 1965 murder has been increasing sharply; last year in some cities it had increased more than 100 percent.

Our age is in the midst of a gigantic revolution . . . and almost always revolution is synonymous with youth. In many countries rebellious college students have literally overthrown governments. Castro was successful in Cuba because he succeeded in inflaming the passions of young people. Mao gathered around himself, in the Peking Red Guard alone, a million Chinese youth.

This generation has experienced revolutions in science, in technology, in education, in space exploration, in religion, in morals. But I'm convinced that the greatest revolution of all is just ahead . . . a spiritual revolution involving young people around the world.

Last fall I traveled through most of the countries of Europe, and I was startled at what I found there. Holland, for example, is filled with hippies and their new brand of morality. (The European hippies prefer to be called Flower People.) It's amazing to see what is happening among the staid, careful Dutch. Many of the older generation refuse to see it. They just will not accept the fact that many of their young people are turning on to a completely different way of life.

The Dutch hippies are reinforced by others from various countries; many of them hitch-hike from as far away as southern France and northern Germany. And in the Netherlands you may find a great many American servicemen who are looking for fun while on leave.

One place many of them look for it is Amsterdam. The first night I was there, I noticed whole sections of the city that were brightly lit late at night. A street through one of these looked like a roadway through a bizarre circus. Hundreds of brightly lighted windows faced the street from what looked like endless storefronts—with a living model behind each picture window. Behind a typical window a smiling girl in a low-cut gown or miniskirt sat on a sofa while revolving lights played on her in constantly changing colors, giving a dazzling fluorescent effect.

From time to time a serviceman or businessman would enter the "shop" and disappear behind a curtain with the girl. In about fifteen minutes she would reappear and wait for her next "customer."

A minister and his wife who had come to Europe with me began walking through one of these districts. The minister left his wife at an intersection while he walked ahead alone, to see how often he would be solicited.

While his wife waited, a prostitute bumped against her and snarled, "Go somewhere else! This is *my* corner!"

All this prostitution is under government license and jurisdiction. Outside of Stockholm, Sweden, I am convinced that Amsterdam is one of the wickedest cities in the world; American cities with all their evil seem almost tame in comparison. Amsterdam brought to my mind this verse of Scripture: "The wicked walk on every side, when the vilest men are exalted" (Psalm 12:8).

I held several youth meetings in the Hague. Four thousand attended the first service. Halfway through the service, a chartered bus pulled up outside the hall we had rented and about forty Flower People emerged. They sauntered inside and plopped down on the floor at the front of the hall. A number of them started playing guitars and mouth organs, while several marched around holding placards. (One of these read "LSD AND LBJ"; I'm still wondering how that one figured in.)

If this confusion had continued, no one would have heard the gospel that night. I called the ushers together and had them escort the hippies out. "This is the house of God," I told them. "This meeting is only for young people who want to find reality. Unless you want that, and unless you refrain from interfering with the work of God, you will have to leave." Ten minutes later, however, I noticed that all these Flower People were back. They had slipped back into the hall quietly, they behaved like ladies and gentlemen, and they listened. When I gave the invitation, the first six to come forward were Flower People.

From Holland I flew to Denmark. Copenhagen shocked me—and I don't shock very easily any more. The covers of books and periodicals in dozens of newsstands pictured the sex act, the details of homosexual and lesbian intercourse, and all kinds of sex perversion—in full color. Brutal acts of sadism and masochism were also shown in intimate detail: sex with whips, with needles, with hot liquids, with punching and biting. It was unbelievable.

I saw many youngsters in their early teens poring over these publications. The Danish Christians, seeing my amazement, told me, "If this shocks you, wait until you get to Sweden." I couldn't imagine anything worse than what I had just seen.

Yet the young people flocked to my meetings in Copenhagen. And some of the things they said had a familiar note: "Our parents don't understand us. They're still living in the shadows of the hardships of the Second World War, and they're only interested in piling up money. They don't understand our needs today at all. And everything we have leaves us bored."

It was a rare privilege to talk straight from the shoulder to these young people, and to lead many of them to the Christ who makes life exciting and wonderful.

I held meetings in Norway and Finland, and in both countries I found the young people taking barbiturates and narcotics, unable to find in either drugs or promiscuity a solution to their restlessness and boredom. The combination of a state church and a socialistic government, I'm afraid, leaves little to stem the tide of depression and suicide in many European countries, and makes it all the more clear that the only final answer to any problem is the living Christ.

The highlight of my trip was Sweden.

I could not imagine that it would be a highlight when I came into Stockholm. The pornography there is unbelievable. I saw a little twelve-year-old girl at a typical newsstand poring over books and magazines that pictured every form of sexual perversion and degeneracy imaginable. And pictures representing these acts were spread out in full color in shop windows, so that children could not help seeing them on the way to school.

I arrived in Stockholm on a Saturday, and on Sunday afternoon I met with Christian leaders who had come from all over Sweden. I thought of my own twelve-year-old daughter being exposed to such filth, and I asked these people why no voice protested such vile pornography. Some of them said that it had built up gradually, and they had come to accept it. They told me that there had been a moral landslide for some time; that the high schools, for example, distributed contraceptive pills, and that premarital sex was openly advocated. These Christian leaders said that they had tried to withstand the landslide of evil for a time, but they had given up. Yet I sensed a feeling of conviction when I talked with these men and women, and I trusted it would bear fruit.

I learned that drug addiction in Stockholm is critical, and the more I found out about that great city the more frightened I became. When I spoke in Stockholm's great Philadelphia Church that night, I felt clearly directed to speak about the moral situation. I reminded the thousands of citizens who sat before me that homosexuality had led to the destruction of the ancient twin cities of Sodom and Gomorrah. "If God doesn't destroy Stockholm and New York for their open immorality," I said, "He will have to bring the people of Sodom and Gomorrah back to life and apologize. In all justice, God cannot tolerate such vileness unless something changes immediately. I see no hope for the world unless there is a genuine spiritual revolution."

Five hundred young people responded to my first altar call. I took them downstairs for counseling and prayer, and they were so ready that it was like lighting a match to dry tinder. So many of these youngsters began smiting their breasts—like the publican in Jesus' parable—and crying to God for mercy, that the sound was like thunder. One minister who was there fell to his own knees and wept like a baby. He sobbed, "It is just like the sound of many waters in the Revelation of St. John." There were confessions of lurid sin, and of coldness toward God.

The next day I saw five hundred young people board trains and buses for their homes and schools and communities, fired with a new zeal to fight pornography, immorality, and atheism. Some went back to pray for their pastors. All Sweden had been touched in some manner in one day.

Soon a great Swedish newspaper published an editorial against pornography. And the editor of another newspaper said that he too was going to take a stand for moral righteousness. He said, "Maybe we can make a mark for what is right after all."

I firmly believe that a moral and spiritual revolution is on the way. As I told people in Stockholm and other cities of Europe, we are in a time of social hemorrhage. Thousands of young people are running away—not just from home, but from God. Our culture is exploding. Moral malignancy will destroy humanity unless something drastic stops it.

The world's hemorrhage cannot be healed without a miraculous act of God. But I have seen God work miracles. I mean real, hard-hitting changes in people's lives—changes so revolutionary and deep that only God could bring them about. And I am convinced that a worldwide miracle is on its way. I have seen the signs in the cities of Europe, in the streets of New York, and in very respectable American communities like Upper Wrexford. . . .

2

Goodniks

"Reverend Mr. Wilkerson?"

The voice at the other end of the telephone was cool and cultured. "This is Ann Gorton of Upper Wrexford. The seven women's circles of First Church would like to invite you to our Autumn Tea exactly one month from today, to speak about your work with delinquent youth. We expect at least three hundred mothers of high-school young people to attend. May we look forward to having you come?"

I checked my schedule and agreed to go.

Upper Wrexford is the name I am going to use for an elite suburban community that supplies many commuters to New York. The town had been much on my mind of late. A number of newspapers and two national magazines had published accounts of teen-age drinking there. It was reported that many parents in Upper Wrexford served their adolescent children alcoholic beverages in their homes. One mother was quoted as saying that the youngsters were going to drink anyhow, and that this way it was done under proper supervision. A father said, "After all, teen-agers have to learn how to handle their liquor." I had referred to this community in some of my talks in other cities, and I wondered whether there was any connection between my references and this invitation.

Apparently there wasn't. Three hundred lovely ladies gathered at First Church at the appointed time, and as I sipped tea I was introduced to wives of advertising men, airline officials, heads of government agencies, businessmen, doctors, lawyers, and all sorts of professional and business leaders. No one mentioned the recent rash of articles about the teen-age drinking in the town.

These wives and mothers listened very politely as I spoke of the crime in the streets of Harlem, the drug addiction in Brooklyn, the delinquency in the Bronx. I sensed a smug feeling, as though the ladies were thinking: *Some of our young people may take a drink or two, but they have nothing in common with the drug addicts and delinquents with whom this man is acquainted.* After I had spoken, I invited any mothers who might be concerned about teen-agers with problems to join me in the prayer room of the church. This seemed to embarrass many of the ladies, but eventually a few joined me in the prayer room.

I took each of these mothers by the hand and said: "If your teen-age son or daughter is in any kind of trouble, I would like to pray for him or her. God answers prayer, and with His help I believe I could help you see your problem and get to the heart of it." They all seemed shocked at my suggestion. One lady said, "I'm sure our teen-agers are all right. They are really very intelligent, and we let them make their own decisions. Certainly they don't have any problems that they can't work through."

The second time I spoke in Upper Wrexford was in

the high school auditorium. More than a thousand teenagers were present. I was sure that many of them were angry at me, for rumors had flown throughout the school that Reverend Wilkerson had bugged these youngsters' mothers, and that I had gone around the country giving their community a bad image. I *had* mentioned the newspaper and magazine stories about Upper Wrexford, but I had no intention of blackening its name; I was simply focusing attention on a known and critical problem. Some of the young people who sat in my audience had come because they thought it would be fun to listen to a fanatic young preacher who claimed he had a cure for drug addiction and boasted that gang leaders were becoming preachers.

The fastbacks and convertibles in the school parking lot confirmed what I knew about my audience that day: These teen-agers were from some of the finest families in America, with the highest IQ's, the best social standing, and the most spending money of any similar group anywhere. They listened attentively as I told of what God was doing in my inner-city parish.

But the real high point of the evening was when I turned the floor over to two converted heroin addicts I had brought with me. Cookie was first. She told this affluent group about growing up in a huge family, all of whom slept in two small rooms in an apartment with holes through the walls. When another baby came along, Cookie's grandmother would pull the drawer out of a dresser to make another crib. Cookie told how her discouraged father had shot himself, how she had always wanted the things other teenagers had, but had never been able to have them.

"But now," Cookie concluded, "all those things

aren't so important to me. I have met Jesus, and He has made my life so full that there's no room for the things I used to long for. Now I have a meaning and a purpose in my life. Now I'm really living!"

Cookie was followed by Denny, who told that group how his drug habit had become so powerful that he had been placed in a state institution. There he had given up so completely that he had tried to hang himself. Before he had succeeded, he had been sent to a hospital where two workers from Teen Challenge met him, brought him back to our home on Clinton Avenue in Brooklyn, and led him to Jesus Christ. Denny's words were often groping and halting, but his voice carried conviction and his face was radiant.

When Denny had finished, I stood up again and said, "If you would like in your life what Cookie and Denny have in theirs, come backstage and see me personally."

I had barely stepped behind the curtain when there was a noise like a stampede. Four hundred young people came barging onto the platform. One group surrounded Cookie, one surged around Denny, and the rest fired questions at me.

I spent nearly two hours listening to confessions the like of which I had never heard. I cannot go into the details, but I wish those cultured mothers at First Church could know some of the things their sons and daughters had been doing, and how guilty and conscience-smitten many of them actually were.

I learned a lot from those high-schoolers. One comment they repeated over and over was this: "My church doesn't reach me any more." From my visits with ministers and church leaders throughout the country I knew that there was a real problem in "holding the young people" almost everywhere, but I was still amazed by the number of young people in Upper Wrexford who made statements like this:

"My church doesn't mean anything to me any more."

"Our minister just doesn't get through to us."

"My church is dead."

"Nobody in my church will answer my questions."

"My religion seems to be a big act with a lot of form and ceremony and rules and regulations. It has no real meaning for me."

"I have never cried in church in my life, but tonight when you spoke I began to cry. I felt something I have never felt before. Before this I don't think Jesus ever really meant anything to me. Why, sir, am I crying?"

Those youngsters shot one question at me after another about Christ, about the end of the world, about God, about the Holy Spirit, especially about eternity. They seemed starved for answers. And they said things like this:

"I guess my preacher is a politician. We get nothing but civil rights and politics Sunday after Sunday."

"My church is good for entertainment and fun, but it sure leaves me cold about God."

"Our church is a sophisticated private club."

"My minister talks so far above my head, I don't think he understands what he is saying himself."

"Our church makes more fuss about its basketball team than anything else."

"The only reason I go to church is because my folks make me, and my girl friend is there."

"There's not a thing in my church that touches me, or stirs me or grabs me or helps me. Sometimes I wish our pastor would make me mad, or yell or scream or do *something* to wake people up."

I've found the same situation as I have toured England, Scotland and Wales. Less than ten percent of the teen-agers in those countries ever attend church. One night I interviewed about two hundred mods and rockers in Bristol, England. One group among them was called the Dossers. It is estimated that there are about nine thousand of these in England; they spend all their time on the move, carrying practically nothing but sleeping bags. Of those two hundred teen-agers, not one had been to church in five years. One young fellow with hair to his shoulders summed up his attitude like this:

"Mr. Wilkerson, why should we get up at seven-thirty in the morning and go to an unheated old barn where the rector reads his part as though the main thing he was interested in was getting out on the golf course?"

Of course, young people are usually very critical of their elders. I have no intention of trying to prove from these criticisms that the church is a lost cause. Yet it seems to me that we who love Christ and His church might listen sympathetically to young people like these and ask ourselves whether there isn't truth in what they are saying.

For example, there is no question in my mind that the gospel of social action preached from so many pulpits today represents lofty ideals and high dreams of social justice. And yet, much of this preaching has grown stale and is no longer reaching young people. One teen-ager after another has told me that he believes very strongly in social involvement—but that he does not think this is all the church should preach.

The one thing that most impressed me about the young people of Upper Wrexford was their evident hunger and thirst for knowledge of the living God. And underneath—sometimes not very far down—I have found this true of a great many members of the new teen-age generation.

One young man greatly interested me. Very well dressed, with tight trousers and slim black shoes, he kept circulating through the whole crowd shouting warnings like this: "Don't get carried away! Don't fall for it, this is just emotionalism. Be objective and use your heads!"

Grandfather Wilkerson used to say, "When you throw a stone into a bunch of dogs, the one that yaps loudest is the one you hit." I was sure that this young man had been hit—and that he was covering it up by launching this tirade. I stopped him and said: "You yourself are carried away. You talk about emotion, but there's plenty of emotion in *your* heart. I think you're ready to admit that you've lost your own objectivity, and you need help! Am I right?"

The young man turned red, and I knew that I had scored a bull's—eye.

A number of the young people who came backstage were there in protest. Their reaction might be summed up like this: "I'm having a ball, life is fun, so please get off my back." One young fellow said, "I like sports, I like parties, I like surfing, I like riding around looking for action. Why can't you let us teen-agers alone? We're not hurting anybody."

This is a fun age, and too many teen-agers are afraid religion will mess up their fun plans; to them, it's something for squares or for people with arthritis or lumbago who can't have fun any more. One young fellow said, "I just can't take a chance on Jesus; it might cost me too much."

Today the girls are prettier, the clothes are sharper, the cars are sportier, money is freer, food is tastier, music is faster, parties are livelier, and dating is easier than ever before. So why should any teen-ager drop out of all this and become a saint?

The answer is amazingly simple. Anyone who wants Christ must be willing to give up the whole world for Him—friends, pleasures, fun, things. But He is absolutely never a killjoy. Lasting, deep joy and happiness, in fact, are impossible without Him. He gives us back, in far greater measure than we had before, everything we really need for fulfillment and satisfaction.

One young fellow at Upper Wrexford said, "Mister Wilkerson, you talk about healing for a broken heart, but my heart has never been broken. You say that Jesus will supply all our needs, but my family treats me all right—I have no needs. The church is supposed to help us find a moral standard, but I've already got a new one. Religion is supposed to relieve our anxieties, but I don't have any. What can God offer me that I don't already have?"

A number of those well-dressed young people revealed a similar attitude. They were not atheists or agnostics, but they seemed to have everything and to have no need for Christ.

Their real need hit me like a bomb when I was in the home of a well-known Christian businessman and his wife. Their young son Jim impressed me; he was so intelligent and well-mannered that I was sure he too must be a Christian. But while I was telling him how much Jesus meant to me, he looked silently at the floor and I suddenly realized that I wasn't getting through.

"Jim," I asked, "have you given your life to Christ?"

I'll never forget his reaction. First Jim looked at his mother as though to say, "Why haven't you talked with me the way this man has?" When she retreated to the kitchen, he let out all his yearning.

"Mister Wilkerson," he said, "Mom and Dad never made religion an issue in our home. Our church doesn't ask for decisions. I have all the allowance I want, a good car of my own, and a lovely girl. I make good grades in school, I'm well adjusted, and I have no real problems. We seem to have everything, sir; I guess we just didn't think we needed anything else."

For years I had been working with young people from the seamy side of the street. The kids in my parish often say that hell is right on their block. One boy said, "If hell is no worse than what I go through every day, I'll gladly go to it." Now, seated in front of me, was a young man who represented a whole generation of teen-agers. They "had everything" and yet did not understand their craving for something greater.

Jim got on his knees with me and asked Christ to

come into his life. When we stood up, he shook hands with me and said:

"Reverend Wilkerson, I hope you can make teenagers all over the country realize how much they do need God. I have a lot of things, but I see now that in reality I've had nothing."

The young person who "has everything" has nothing that will last. What he does need is forgiveness of sin (for everyone has sinned and broken God's laws); confidence in the day of judgment (for we must all eventually face God); and the joy of living each moment with Christ. For life is empty or wonderful as Christ is in it.

I know. When I was young, like a lot of boys everywhere, I was sometimes a little ashamed of "religion," and I too had to fight out my own personal struggle, whether to give my whole self to God. But I was lucky when I was a boy. I didn't "have everything," but I did have God in my home—and I had Grandfather.

3

*The Gospel According
to Grandfather*

People who have read *The Cross and the Switchblade* often ask me to tell them more about Grandfather Wilkerson. They remember the Independence Day weekend when he dropped some sparkler powder near his pulpit, and had the sparks flying and the smoke rising around him as he preached about hell.

Grandfather would have one thing very much in common with today's switched-on generation. He loved noise. When he led a song service, he would get out an old tambourine that he used to rattle and shake like a professional in the Salvation Army. "Pull out all the stops!" he would shout, and before long everyone in his congregation would do just that. As often as not he would start marching around the church or tent during a hymn, and the whole congregation would fall in behind him until everyone within three blocks knew that someone loved God enough to tell the world.

One of my fondest memories of Granddad is the time he came to my father's church when I was only about nine years old. At that time many of the members seemed to be rather proud that they were getting accepted in our community, almost as though they didn't belong to a church that emphasized revivals and the fire of the Spirit. Our church was getting nearly as sedate and quiet as the other churches in town, and some of the folks were worried when they learned that Granddad, who had quite a reputation as a noisy evangelist, was going to hold some services right in our church.

I'll never forget that night he first walked into the pulpit and stretched out his lanky frame to its full six feet of height and looked over our congregation. Granddad had an uncanny way of knowing what was in a person's mind, and I'm sure he knew what a lot of our people were thinking as he looked them over. The silence was eloquent.

Then Grandfather spread his long arms as high and wide as he could reach and he yelled at the top of his voice: "Well, glory, folks! God is here tonight!"

And before he left town, a lot of our sedate church members had learned all over again what it meant to be filled with the Spirit of the living God.

I can't feel much sympathy with ministers who condemn their young people for exchanging a dry, dead church service for a session of rock 'n roll. Under the spell of such music, teen-agers have been seen wriggling, screaming, weeping, raising their arms, contorting their faces and bodies with intense feeling, and simply letting go—in release of all their pent-up emotions. Grandfather knew that everyone has a heart as well as a head, that the first and greatest commandment is to *love* God with all we have, and that the kind of enthusiasm young people work up today for the Beatles and the Rolling Stones belongs in the church. Weeping, intense feeling, and the response of the whole person—body, soul, and spirit—is a purely religious experience. It should be properly channeled and controlled, and directed toward the Lord.

Grandfather came to Bellerose, Long Island, before that town had a name, to hold a revival. He pitched his tent there on the outskirts of Queens on a wooden platform that had previously been used by a circus; the huge calliope had been left behind, and filled the center of the platform, its enormous pipes stretching clear up into the top of the tent. Grandpa preached the first night to a total audience of fifteen ladies, all dressed in white. He always put all the energy he had into a revival meeting, and each day he visited in the community, inviting people to the services. The second night, however, only the same little group came to his tent, and this continued for two long weeks. By and large, people were a little afraid to attend; they had heard stories about the Reverend J. A. Wilkerson.

People said that Granddad sometimes got so mad at the devil, during his tent services, that he would take off his coat and throw it at him. If that didn't get any results, he would take off a shoe and toss that, too. The stories were true. Granddad was more interested in results than conventional behavior, and in the end he always got a crowd. And he got results.

That particular July, Grandfather became so blessed that he began to shinny up one of the pipes on the calliope, and somehow he got stuck near the top of the tent. A heckler in the crowd called the fire department, and word spread fast that something amazing was happening over at the revival tent. When the fire truck arrived, four hundred onlookers came with it. To this day no one seems to be sure whether Grandfather was really stuck or not. Grandfather was satisfied that he had his crowd, and before they left he was preaching to all of them.

I believe there are still oldtimers in Nashville, Tennessee, who remember the time J. A. Wilkerson brought his streetcar to a stop right in the middle of town. While he was in his twenties he worked as a streetcar conductor to earn a living and preached in his off hours to save sinners. Grandfather was one of the first conductors to run a streetcar with airbrakes. When his car stopped in the heart of Nashville, he climbed up on the roof and fiddled around for half an hour, apparently looking for the source of the trouble. When the crowd of curious bystanders grew large enough, Grandpa stood up on top of his streetcar pulpit and began preaching the Gospel.

No one ever went to sleep in one of Reverend J. A. Wilkerson's services. More than once he was known to go into the congregation, when someone present looked the least bit sleepy, and walk right up to that startled saint. Very gently but firmly Grandfather would lift him from his seat and walk him back to the pulpit. Then, a strong hand on the man's arm, he would walk back and forth across the platform with him while he finished his sermon. Grandfather's methods got around, and he had the most wide-awake congregations in North America.

When Grandfather preached, no one could doubt that he knew what he was talking about. He became a Christian the hard way. He struggled against being saved when he was a young man, and finally left the Southern community where he knew people were praying for him. Grandfather took a bus all the way to Olivet, Illinois, where he decided to look for a job, far from his meddling friends. But as he got off the bus he found himself looking at a barn on which someone had painted a message in letters three feet high: PREPARE TO MEET THY GOD.

"Oh, my God," cried Grandfather, "can't I get away from this anywhere?"

That cry turned out to be a prayer. Grandpa, realizing he could not get away from God, gave in, and turned his life over to Him.

At that time he had tuberculosis and cirrhosis of the liver. This was simply one more challenge to the little group of believers who brought James Wilkerson to the throne of grace. They believed in a God big enough to handle a man's lungs and liver, and they passed that faith on to James. After his friends had put their hands on his diseased body and had joined with him in a simple prayer of faith, the tuberculosis and cirrhosis disappeared. Grandfather enjoyed a long life and good health throughout a very energetic ministry.

So Grandfather spoke from experience when he talked about the power of an all-powerful God. He became famous for his healing ministry. He knew that the Great Physician could do for anyone else what He had done for him, and he sent out committed men and women in teams of two or three to the homes of the sick. They would read the promises of Scripture, lay their hands on the sufferers' bodies, and pray. Time after time, the sickness would disappear. Even cancer yielded to the prayer of faith from Grandfather and his workers.

Grandfather was poorly educated by today's standards. He read few books, but he knew the Bible and God, and he loved people. College presidents drove for miles to hear his wit and wisdom, and theological students sometimes had to hang their heads in shame as he drove the sword of the Lord into their cold, back-slidden hearts.

Grandpa was a master psychologist. He filled his sermons with illustrations, humor, and pathos; his hearers gasped, laughed, and wept as he spoke. He often made use of simple homely things in his messages. When he was asked where he got all his illustrations, he would usually say, "They just come to me from nowhere. The Spirit of God fills my mouth when I open it in faith, and I give Him all the praise and the glory."

Grandfather Wilkerson was holding a camp meeting on the outskirts of one city near a chicken farm when a hen walked into the tent and onto the platform where he was praying. During the prayer the hen laid an egg not far from the pulpit. Then she stretched her wings and cackled proudly.

"Look at that!" said Grandfather. "She's praising God for being able to lay that beautiful brown egg. My friends, this hen doesn't know the first thing about salvation, but she opens her mouth in praise to the Lord. Some of you are ashamed to throw up your hands and jump to your feet when the Lord blesses you with the magnitude of all His love, but this hen praises her Creator with her whole body. And you folks are too sedate and stiff and proud to do what this hen can do."

Grandfather brought up his children by the Bible.

It would probably shock a lot of present-day parents, educators, and psychology-conscious young people, but he believed in woodshed revival; he spared the rod as rarely as he spoiled the child. Today if either a parent or a teacher dares to use a switch or a paddle, school psychologists are likely to mutter about mental scars and childhood traumas. But a little more of Granddad's medicine might prevent a lot of permanent scars on youthful souls and spirits.

Now, years later, psychiatry is beginning to learn that Granddad was not mistaken in the idea that young persons should make a daily contribution to the duties of the home without expecting payment, and thus learn responsibility. (For example, by getting an outside job such as a paper route or lawn-mowing, and contributing something to the family income from their earnings.) Grandfather didn't know these things instinctively; he got them straight from the Bible. He got other things from the same Book: family prayers and the cultivation of faith and piety from childhood. He led his family in daily devotions, reading from a well-worn leather Bible—not a Bible story book. Today nearly all his ten children are busy in Christian work.

If Granddad could see the hippies of today, he would be amused and amazed. I'm sure he would say that what these young rebels need is a trip to the barbershop, a razor strop to the posterior, and a dose of regular attendance at a good church. To some, this is an oversimplification. Yet two thousand years of experience, in thousands of Christian homes, in every kind of culture and climate, witness to this truth: When a child is properly raised in a Christian home and taught Biblical morality, he rarely has to be re-formed in jail.

If Grandfather were preaching today, I am sure that he would be called a prude, a square, and a fanatic. He preached against cigarettes, cards, dirty books, and vile imaginations. He believed that when you had Christ in your heart, you loved your enemies, you treated your wife decently, you cared about your children, and you quit kicking the dog. He preached complete consecration. He told people they should come to church "prayed up," with a song or a testimony that would build up other people.

At one time when Grandpa Wilkerson was pastor of a church in Mansfield, Ohio, a number of the members were in an apathetic mood. They prayed halfheartedly at one prayer meeting that the fire of God would fall and that people would get the fire. In the midst of this a wonderful Negro lady who was a member got to her feet and said, her face radiant:

"I didn't come to get the fire, I brought the fire with me! Hallelujah!"

Grandfather liked people who brought the fire with them. The members of his congregations worked for God all week, praying for the sick and taking baskets of food to the unemployed and needy. Then when Sunday came, they had so much to testify to that they had to wait their turn. In Grandfather's testimony meetings, five or six different people often got to their feet at once in their eagerness to speak.

Granddad set an example of generosity himself, although few people ever knew about it. Very often he

would quietly leave some food or a suit or some
money with a poor family, and he tried to do it in
such a way that no one learned where the gift came
from.

I believe many young people today would particu-
larly admire Grandfather's directness and sincerity.
He used to say that it is better to be a red-hot delinquent than a make-believe saint. I have heard him
quote from memory these words: *I know thy works,
that thou art neither cold nor hot: I would thou wert
cold or hot. So then because thou art lukewarm, and
neither cold nor hot, I will spew thee out of my
mouth* (Revelation 3:15-16). The greatest sin of all,
he contended, was lukewarmness. His preaching was
direct and straight, and everyone knew that he meant
and lived what he said.

Grandfather had a son named Kenneth who married my mother, Ann. At times, early in their marriage, Mother would get upset after some of Grandfather's sermons. What he said applied directly to
what she was thinking and doing that she was sure
Kenneth must have talked to his father about her.
Later she realized that spiritual insight was Grandfather's special gift. He knew people, and he was so
completely surrendered that God could speak right
through him.

The young people responded to Grandfather's
preaching, as I am sure many of them would today.
He loved them, and challenged them. "Use your
gifts," he would tell them; he urged them to enter the
ministry or some other work in which they could be
truly useful. And Grandfather made good use of

young people in his work. He held many meetings in parks and on street corners. These were usually conducted from the back of an old truck which he drove to the scene overflowing with young people. They would sing, play various instruments, and tell what God had done in their lives. This made a powerful impact on the young people who came to look and listen.

If Grandfather were here today, what would he say to our young people? I know he wouldn't accept the phony excuses I hear from some of them. Often a young drug addict will explain to me that he's hooked because of "sibling rivalries" or "interpersonal relationships" or something similar. He tends to blame his problem on the fact that society has failed him, the church hasn't reached him, and his kindergarten teacher mistreated him.

A young homosexual is likely to read all the literature on sexual deviation and blame his mother. A juvenile delinquent finds it easy to blame his misdeeds on the fact that his father never took him to the ball game. Unwed mothers blame the unwed fathers—and *they* always say, "She led me on." Kids who lose their faith blame the science or biology teacher.

I think Grandfather would say that this is the old story of Adam blaming Eve and Eve accusing Adam, and that everyone has the "blaming blues." I believe he would tell a great many young people this:

"Quit looking for a scapegoat! Quit passing the buck. It's time you stopped looking for someone else to blame your troubles on. Take a good look in the mirror and be honest with yourself. Grow a back-

bone and tell yourself a thousand times a day, *It's up
to me. No more free rides.* Grow up! And don't be
afraid of prayer, or faith, or God."

4

Poor Dad

Our church wasn't *across* the tracks while I was in high school; it was underneath them. The church where Dad was minister at that time was really a big old house that had been more or less altered to hold a congregation in the spacious built-on extension room. And trains often passed over it on a high trestle.

Just about the time Dad would start the Sunday service, a train would usually rumble overhead. The floor would vibrate, the windows would shake, and soot would seep through the windows. That was usually Dad's cue to announce a hymn. I remember smelling the soft coal smoke while we sang "Amazing Grace, How Sweet the Sound"—but most of the sound in *my* ears was the clank and roar of a freight train or an express hurtling along the elevated track above us.

Another time when it seemed a train never failed to come along was right in the middle of the sermon. Dad had a good voice, but he knew better than to wear out his lungs competing with the Pennsylvania Railroad. Sometimes he would stop right there and wait. The people would smile sympathetically and

shake their heads; it was about the only way to com-
municate at such a time, and it gave us all a chance
for some silent communion in the middle of the service. I think maybe it was good for us all to have this
common problem at the heart of our church service.
But sometimes a train would vibrate overhead when
Dad wasn't of a mind to stop in the middle of what he
was saying. Then he would keep right on going, out-
shouting the train, and it put real emphasis into his
words.

I didn't appreciate my church at all, though, the
day Tim Ashcroft stopped me at our high school.

"Hey, David," he said, "don't you belong to that
church down under the railroad tracks?"

Timothy was a member of the student council, and
he had never shown any great interest in either me or
my church before this. I wondered why he was interested in it now. I soon found out.

"Yeah," I said. "That's my church."

"Well, that's great. You see, the student council is
visiting various churches, to learn how various groups
worship, and we want to visit yours. Do you have a
service Sunday night?"

"Yeah." I didn't feel very enthusiastic about the leading members of our student body coming to my
church.

"Eight o'clock?"

I had a sudden temptation to say "Yeah" again. If
they got there at eight, they wouldn't see or hear so
many of the things that began to make me feel very
embarrassed as I thought about our church. But I
couldn't tell a deliberate lie.

"It usually starts about seven-thirty."

"Good. We'll be there at seven-thirty. Say, isn't your dad the preacher there?"

"Yeah."

"We'll be there Sunday night. By the way, I hear you people climb the walls down there."

I knew what he meant. The members of our church were known as Holy Rollers, and there were rumors that we jumped, yelled, rolled in the aisles, and behaved like acrobats in a circus during our services. The trouble was that it wasn't all rumor. I felt like crawling in a hole as Tim walked away. I could feel my cheeks burning.

I knew that Dad was a man of God, and he had always been the best father in the world to me, but as I thought of my high-school friends coming to our church and listening to one of his sermons, I began to feel ashamed. Dad was self-educated. My science teacher would have been horrified if he had heard Dad talk about Genesis or heaven in such literal terms.

I didn't tell anyone what I had learned, but all the rest of the week I worried about what was going to happen Sunday night. Finally, Sunday afternoon, I sidled into Dad's study and told him the news. I said, "I hope it will be a dignified meeting."

Dad didn't say anything, and I tried to explain.

"I mean, it's going to be quite a thing to have the student council come, and they probably aren't used to churches like ours."

Dad kept looking at me in a kindly way, and I felt that I wasn't communicating.

"What I mean is, it would be too bad if folks got too excited, wouldn't it? The student council fellows probably wouldn't understand it. And I hope you won't raise your voice too much tonight, Dad. They might think you were shouting. Especially if a train comes through—don't you think you ought to wait till it's gone instead of outpreaching it this time?"

I knew that I wasn't getting very far, but I kept trying. I tried to get the idea across to Dad that he should preach with as much polish as possible, and that he ought to use some big words to make a good impression.

I remembered how Sister Leah often felt blessed in the middle of a service, and I told Dad I hoped he wouldn't let her get excited. I remembered how easily she could get started shouting or crying. I devoutly hoped she wouldn't do either.

Dad kept on smiling kindly at me until I was all through. I knew he was hurt, although he tried not to show it. When I had finished, he said, "Thank you for telling me this, David. I intend to let God have His way."

I was in church that night at six-thirty, dusting furniture, lining up all the hymn books so they were evenly spaced in each pew, and making sure every seat was clean and every aisle neat.

At seven-thirty the usual number of members was there, including Sister Leah, and the usual four-minute train rumbled overhead. No sign of the student council! I was greatly relieved, and I prayed.

"Please, dear God, don't let them show up."

No sooner had I thought that prayer than in swaggered Tim Ashcroft and four other members of our high-school student council. They smilingly settled in a back pew as Dad announced the second hymn. I was on pins and needles, hoping Sister Leah wouldn't get too blessed and take off with a few hallelujahs, but she didn't, and I was thankful that nothing undignified had happened by the end of the hymn.

Then chorus time arrived. This was the time our folks really got blessed. They believed in the verse, "Make a joyful noise unto God" (Psalm 66:1). And they clapped their hands as they sang, in accordance with the admonition in Psalm 47:1—"O clap your hands, all ye people; shout unto God with the voice of triumph."

We sang "Honey in the Rock," and by the second stanza everyone was clapping and making a joyful noise—everyone but our visitors and me. I slid down into my seat, afraid to take even a peek at the fellows in the back row.

Sister Leah got blessed, and so did nearly everyone else. As we sang, someone cried "Amen!" and then amens and hallelujahs filled the room. Sister Leah got to her feet, waved a white handkerchief, and shouted at the top of her voice, "Glory!" At the piano, Sister Ruth pounded louder than I had ever heard her, and as she played she sobbed and shouted, "Praise God!"

I tried to sink out of sight.

Suddenly my father got to his feet and held his hand high. When there was silence he said quietly, "Let us pray."

Never have I heard anyone pray with more depth and sincerity. Dad prayed for the youth of this nation;

he prayed for the sons and daughters of parents who had gone astray; he prayed for wisdom as a father. What he said was simple, I suppose, but it had a kind of spiritual and intellectual depth that made me ashamed of my self-pity and my pride. Suddenly my father loomed before me as a man of God. In fact, I forgot myself as I became conscious of the majesty and the power of God. I saw the greatness of Dad's life, dedicated to the cause of reaching lost humanity. Tears began to trickle down my cheeks, and I bowed my head and asked God to forgive the shameful attitude I had had toward the man who had brought us into His very presence.

When Dad had finished praying, he began to preach. By now, I couldn't care less what my high-school acquaintances thought. I forgot they were there, as I drank in the message; I felt like a desert traveler who has come at last to an oasis filled with clear cold water.

That night I apologized to Dad before I went to bed. I tried to tell him what he had done for me, and I was surprised that he seemed to understand exactly the battle I had gone through.

The next morning I braced myself as I settled into the first class at high school. I was prepared for the worst. Just before the final bell rang, Tim Ashcroft called across the room to me.

"Dave," he said, a warm smile on his face, "that was a good meeting last night. Your Dad doesn't fool around. I wish my minister had that much courage. And the folks in your church sure enjoy their religion! Mind if we come again?"

A generation ago the average church was far different from the typical church today. Most churches had no public address systems, no wall-to-wall carpeting, no recessed lighting, no perimeter heating nor air conditioning, no spacious education units and recreation halls, In fact, the churches I was used to were usually down by the railroad tracks and often near the slums. The clapboards on the old frame building let the heat out and the cold in, and the pot-bellied stove warmed only one side of a person at a time. The carpet might be an old tarpaper runner up the main aisle, with a strip of old used carpeting nailed down in front of the old wooden altar rail. The heads of those nails never would stay down; their only purpose seemed to be to snag the trousers and dresses of those who knelt in prayer.

The parking lot in front of a typical old time church looked like a junkyard, with old black Model A's and Chevvies with rumble seats. The piano was an upright that sounded like a honky-tonk instrument. Wires were strung all over the ceiling so that the single main room could be subdivided for Sunday school by pulling drapes into position. Whenever another room was needed, more wire was strung up and another drape was hung. The rest room was a little outhouse in the back yard, and only the brave and desperate tried to reach it through the ice and snow.

In those days the church roof often leaked, the water pipes froze, the floorboards creaked, and the old wooden pews had been painted and repainted over and over. The hymnals were worn, and in many churches people often sang from memory. They knew a good many of those Gospel songs and hymns by heart.

Sunday night was a big night; there was no television to keep people out of God's house. The Sunday night services tended to be especially lively—people didn't look around in amazement or cringe when someone shouted, "Hallelujah!"

Those were the days when it was an event to have a missionary come to church. Workers from Africa, China, India, or the islands of the sea would tell of their experiences, and young people would be fired with desire to follow in their footsteps. The missionaries would leave behind them young men and women possessed with a call from God to go out, as they had done, into the uttermost parts of the earth to preach the gospel. The great mission stations that have been established all around the globe can be traced back to that time of fire and glory and earnest dedication.

Soul-winning was a way of life in those days, and young people were often busy working for God. There was little time for foolishness and little chance to complain about nothing to do. There were few instruction classes on how to win souls, there were no training manuals or special techniques, but the workers were so filled with the love of God that they were able to disarm and break down resistance through an innate simplicity and directness. There were few committees or commissions then, and few books on "How to Do It," but the work got done anyway.

In my father's and grandfather's time, the man who stood in the pulpit spoke with the conviction, "Thus

saith the Lord." Young people knew that their minister was in touch with God. They knew him as a man
of prayer, not as a personality boy or an entertainer or
a professional. He was not just the man who kept the
bills paid or conducted weddings, baptisms and fu-
nerals. His influence came not so much from what he
preached as from how he preached it and how he
lived.

The preacher's words could cut and hurt, but he
also knew how to love and to heal. He watched over
the young people in his church; he tried to keep mis-
takes and grudges from spoiling their lives, and to
pull the roots of bitterness and cynicism out of their
hearts. He preached faith and trust, and he believed
that God could meet every need.

I'm not suggesting that we go back to the past. I
don't want to, and no one should try to. We are living
today in the greatest period of opportunity in history,
and God has put us here for such a time as this. There
may be much that we can't accept from the old days,
but that is no reason to throw out the baby with the
bath water. In spite of all the changes since my Dad's
day, his age was *basically* little different from ours.
Human nature is the same, human problems are the
same, and God is the same.

When anyone tells me that the old gospel doesn't
work any more, and that we should try something different, I understand a little better how Dad must have
felt that Sunday I tried to make things more dignified.
I know how important it is to let God get through to
people, to let God have His way.

For the greatest experience any person, young or

old, can have is a realization of the presence of God—in love and forgiveness and redeeming power.

I know.

old, can have is a realization of the presence of

5

"Jesus Saves—
Green Stamps"

God called me to work for Him when I was eleven
years old. That summer I went to a youth camp on a
work scholarship—my folks couldn't afford the tu-
ition. I had a horrible time. The other kids called me
"Skinny" or "Preacher's Kid," and they made fun of
my thick glasses. When everyone chose sides for a
game, no one wanted Skinny. I remember once when
six of us hadn't been picked for either side in a base-
ball game. Bud Impesivo, who was a crack athlete but
who seemed to me at that time the world's worst
bully, yelled, "We'll take these five if you'll take Skinny!"

That's the way it went all through camp. I had
come there hoping to have a change from school,
where I had been getting poor grades in class and a
rough time after hours, but it was even worse at
camp. I wondered why I had come.

I found out the last night. There was a special evening service, and all of a sudden the speaker seemed
to be talking only to me.

"I don't care who you are," he said, "God wants
you. I don't care how big you are, or how young. I

don't care how skinny you are, or how poor your grades may be in school."

That grabbed me. I listened with every ounce of attention when he went on, "All God wants from you is a willing heart. He wants to hear you say, 'Here am I. Use me!'"

When the speaker invited the young campers forward to give their lives to Christ, I ran down that aisle and knelt down and raised my hands above my head as far as I could reach, and I cried at the top of my voice, "Jesus, I'm nothing, but I want You to use me. Take what I have. It's all yours."

That night a fire from God began to burn in my soul, and I knew that I would never again be the same. After that, many a time when the other kids were playing, I was praying. While they were watching movies or reading comics, I was seeking God or reading the Bible. I had learned that my life had a purpose and a mission, and this I have never lost sight of.

My parish is tough. In one police precinct near Teen Challenge Center, there are three times as many murders as there were ten years ago. In a main precinct of Greenwich Village there are more rapes than in the whole state of Delaware and more murders than in all South Dakota. Some of the young hippies I see throw four-letter words to the heavens as though they are daring God to respond. One young fellow had a picture of Jesus embroidered on the back of his leather jacket. At the top of the picture were the words "Jesus Saves." Underneath it—"Green Stamps."

Many of the young men and women who come to us have been brought up almost from babyhood on

hate, fear, sex, dope, perversion, and violence. I know
young hoodlums who have stabbed innocent victims,
robbed banks, mugged old ladies, fought for their
lives in gang rumbles, and dodged policemen's bullets;
I have seen them. Yet I have seen these same charac-
ters shake like leaves, cry like babies, and fall on their
faces begging for mercy when the Spirit of God
stripped off their false front of toughness and exposed
what they really were—lonely sinners desperately
searching for happiness and peace.

I believe there are young rebels all over the nation
who use the same kind of tough front to hide their
real selves. These youngsters talk big, and they often
pretend to be No. 1 big shots. They are would-be Liz
Taylors and Frank Sinatras, and from their talk you
wonder whether they have outdone even those two.
They try to make you think they're tough as nails. But
it's often a real false front.

The first time I saw Mary Furcolo, it was obvious
she was pregnant. She was only sixteen, and I knew
she was from a good family in a typical suburban
community. She had come to my office for an interview, hoping we would take her into our Girls' Home
until her baby was born. And from the way she
dressed and acted, it looked as though she was proud
of her pregnancy.

"Who's the father of your baby?" I asked her.

Mary snickered and shrugged her shoulders boast-
fully. "I dunno, Rev. I ran around with so many boy-
friends, it coulda been anyone!"

But two weeks later, when I met Mary in the hallway of the Home, she hung her head and there were
tears in her eyes.

"Pastor," she said, "I'm so ashamed. Since I've been here I've really learned for the first time how much I've sinned.

"When I first got pregnant," she went on, "I was actually proud of it. My friends gave me real respect. And I wanted to keep my cool, because I figured that showed real class.

"But your chapel services and your workers have really got through to me. It isn't funny any more. I feel nothing but anguish over what I did. I know God has forgiven me now, but I want you to forgive me too—if you can—for the smart aleck way I acted when I came here."

Mary hung her head even lower. "The truth is . . . I wasn't all that popular."

I understood. And I understand the other calloused-fronters who try to impress me with their bigshot misdeeds. Enough of it is real, but a lot of it is a cover-up. When these boys and girls find God, they understand immediately that they can't impress Him, and all their phoniness begins to crumble.

This came home to me very clearly when I was a speaker at a banquet for young people in Rhode Island. The banquet was about to begin when the back door suddenly opened, and in pranced a tall lad followed by two other boys. From the way they were dressed and walked, I pegged the first as a gang leader and the others as two of his followers. The three of them coolly scanned the entire scene, then headed straight for the front of the banquet hall. At one of the tables near mine were six very attractive teen-age girls, and these three boys had no intention of escaping their notice. They walked with exaggerated steps clear to the front of the hall, eyed the girls with obvious delight, and then went on around to the only remaining seats, near the door they had entered.

Sitting across from me was José, a former heroin addict who was now a Teen Challenge associate. José leaned toward me and whispered, "Pastor, you want me to get hold of those guys and give them the word to behave, or shall I pick them up and carry them out?"

"No," I said, "let them alone. That's what I'm here for, to reach fellows like that. God is able to get hold of their hearts, let's leave them in His hands."

For a while I regretted having said that. All during the meal, this gang leader and his friends kept finding it necessary to make trips to the wash room—which was conveniently near the six girls' table. No less than four times they found occasion to visit it, and each time they grinned and winked at the girls as they passed by, swinging their hips.

When I started to speak at the close of the meal, I couldn't help thinking: *These fellows don't want God. They are tough and hard, and they don't even have the courtesy of a good many of the slum kids in Harlem or the Bowery.*

At the end of my message I gave an invitation to accept Christ, as I usually do when I speak to a group of young people. No one present could have been more surprised than I at the first ones on their feet. They were the three gang members, and they came straight to my table. This time there was no hip-swinging or girl-watching. They put their hands on the white cloth covering my table and their leader said, "Mr. Wilkerson, we need God. Pray for us right now."

From that moment the three boys seemed to forget the crowd and the girls. Very earnestly they questioned me, and when they dropped to their knees I was convinced that they were being completely honest—perhaps for the first time in their lives. All the nonchalance had been a phony front to cover three hearts that were lonely, sad, and in desperate need of help.

I'll never forget the day Phil walked into our Center. He was in his late twenties, and everything about him looked as tough as his record. He had been on various drugs for years, and had robbed, mugged, and beat up a number of people to get his narcotics. He had spent a lot of time in prison and looked like one of the Untouchables. When he walked into the Center, his swagger seemed to say, "Don't breathe on me. I'm a real swinger."

As soon as Phil was inside the building, Nicky Cruz walked up to him and said, "You stink." Phil was probably more startled than he had ever been in his life. "Mister," Nicky went on, "we're going to have a chapel service in a few minutes. If you want help, get into that chapel. Sit in the back, be quiet, and listen."

Phil obeyed like a first-grader the first day in Sunday school. During that chapel service, three young drug addicts testified to being clean—and Phil knew they were telling the truth because he used to shoot drugs on nearby rooftops with two of them. Another young man who testified was one with whom Phil had spent time in jail. These were miracles, and he knew it.

What completely unnerved Phil, however, was what he heard from the young man who preached in that chapel service. As he talked about sin, Phil thought: *How in the world does that young fellow know all about me? Somebody musta told him I was coming, becuase he's ratting on me right down the line.*

The speaker invited any addicts present to stand up, come forward, kneel down at the altar, and confess their sins, and Phil was the first to respond. As soon as he fell on his knees, all the swaggering rebellion seemed to ooze out of him like water out of a sponge. His hands shot up in the air, reminding me of the publican in Jesus' story who smote his breast and cried, "God have mercy on me, a sinner." In fact, those were Phil's very words.

God answered.

It may sound too simple to say, "Christ is the Answer" in our sophisticated age, but the wonderful fact is that Christ *is* the answer to the questions and the deepest problems of youth today.

After a national magazine did an article on drug addiction, eighteen-year-old Joan Ferraris of Springfield, Pennsylvania, wrote the editor:

"I may be crazy and a little foolish, but I'm not dumb enough to get hooked on drugs. Hippies may find me square, but I'd rather soothe my problems with an old-fashioned prayer than a wild trip to nowhere."

So would I.

"I'm glad she returned," I said wonderingly why he had

6

Freakout on Life

Dr. Terry looked like a prosperous businessman; actually he was the president of a midwestern college. I couldn't imagine at first why he had come to my office at Teen Challenge Center. Then he took a manila envelope from his briefcase, drew from it a whole stack of photographs, and pushed them toward me.

The pictures were all of an attractive, teen-age girl. Her hair hung long and straight and a bit uncombed, and she wore beads around her neck, and bracelets on wrists and ankles.

"Mr. Wilkerson," this college president said in an agitated voice, "this is my daughter Cynthia. She is only fifteen. She is a lovely girl, Mr. Wilkerson. She was always at the top of her class. My wife and I love her, and we've always done everything in our power to make her happy and well adjusted. But she has run away from home!

"Several months ago," he continued, "Cynthia vanished. We hired detectives to trace her and discovered she had flown to San Francisco and was living in the Haight-Ashbury section there. She refused to come home! I had to fly to San Francisco myself and I actually had to bribe her to come back with me."

"I'm glad she returned," I said, wondering why he had come to Teen Challenge. "A lot of young people leave home these days and don't go back."

"But she wouldn't stay!" His voice was nearing the breaking point. "In just five weeks she vanished again. I don't understand it! Cynthia had no reason to leave home. We are convinced that she's now in New York, hiding somewhere in Greenwich Village. Mr. Wilkerson, would you pass her pictures among your workers there and ask them to look for her? If any of them ever see her, my wife and I have just one message for Cynthia: Please tell her we love her and want her to come home."

Dr. Terry's eyes were wet, and we separated with heavy hearts. Soon afterward I distributed the pictures of Cynthia among the workers at our Greenwich Village coffeehouse, The Lost Coin at 190 Sullivan Street, and I passed on Dr. Terry's message. But we never found Cynthia Terry.

To me, Cynthia represents a whole generation of young people today. You can see so many of them in the Village these days. As I walked through that part of New York recently, I passed a dozen young men with fringed leather jackets and tousled hair, some of them wearing earrings, who sang boisterously as they worked their way down the narrow street from one bar to another. Two young girls in miniskirts passed me hand in hand. A stubbly-faced drunk weaved uncertainly across the street, scrambling out of sight as a policeman approached on horseback. A young white girl came out of a coffeehouse with her Negro "date." The streets and cafes were filled with curly-haired, bearded youths, lank-haired girls, barefooted hippies whose sex was hard to guess, sidewalk artists, and youngsters in every kind of dress imaginable. You name it, and you'll see it in Greenwich Village.

Some of these young people, I realized thankfully, would sooner or later drop into The Lost Coin, where they would receive the help they are unconsciously looking for. But what, I wondered, would become of all the great numbers who would never go there, who would keep on wandering through the dark byways of the Village in their fruitless search?

Young people constantly crowd into the Village cafes and bars, pour into basement hangouts, line up in front of entertainment spots where an Off-Off-Broadway play or a Happening is going on, or just roam the streets. These young people flock to lower Manhattan from all over the country, and in recent months more and more of them have been crowding in. They let their hair grow, find sleeping space in some rented room—often amid quite a large group of hippies of both sexes—and start living what looks to them like a dream life. Their goal is absolute freedom, and they come very close to reaching it. It does not take any of them long to find that free food and fun are usually available somewhere, and that there is almost no limit to the kinds of experimentation that are possible.

The hippies move from bar to bar and from one night spot to another, reveling in the chaos of their new life. With all the usual restraints gone, they live for thrills—in music, art, dancing, drinking, dope and sex. Free love, constantly talked about, becomes an umbrella for all kinds of immorality.

The Village has for generations been a haven for

nonconformists and restless spirits seeking freedom and fulfillment. But what is most disturbing to me about this current migration is the *youth* of the people involved. Especially the girls. Most of the ones I see are so tragically young, some barely into their teens. They are attractive, even in the bizarre clothes they wear; they are well educated. They come from "good" families. And most of their parents don't have the slightest idea why their daughters have run away from home.

The boys they find themselves among are usually older, and considerably more blasé. They talk a line of philosophy, freedom and distorted psychology that intoxicates these girls, who at first, despite their surface sophistication, have a terrible innocence. But that gets knocked off quickly. As one of these girls said, "I'd meet boys, and I'd *love* them. But they'd just use me, and then they'd say, 'Good-bye, now; that's it.' And that hurt."

On Saturdays and Sundays the Village overflows with "weekend hippies," young people who come in regularly from respectable suburban areas of Connecticut, New York and New Jersey. I often wonder whether their parents don't know or don't care where they are and what they are doing.

There is always a great deal doing in Greenwich Village, for that area of the city never sleeps. In the afternoons the parks in Washington Square and Tompkins Square are filled with youngsters playing everything from bongo drums and guitars to chess and records. They dance. They clap. They smoke marijuana. They just roam about. When night comes, glaring neon signs draw them to the Dom and the Electric Circus on St. Mark's Place, to Off-Broadway shows, to coffeehouses and bars with various degrees of offbeat entertainment, to Off-Off-Broadway. At the latter—at such places as Cafe Engage on East Tenth Street, the Bridge on East Eighth Street, and Cafe La Mama—anything may happen, and often does.

According to a reporter who visited a Village dance hall, "Everything is designed to attack the senses and break down inhibitions." One of the bouncers there agreed. "The girls here dance at you until you pick them up," he said. "I've never seen anything like this." That is the estimate made of this current "youth subculture" by two men you might expect to be hardened to anything. But here has never been anything quite like this before, even in the Village.

Take a look at Orky. He lives on East Seventh Street, a young man with shoulder-length hair who has something of a reputation for sheltering runaway teen-agers and persuading some of them to return home. Orky's apartment is open to almost anyone who wants a bed or a shower. Most of the time about twenty-five Diggers live there. The Diggers are a special kind of hippie with an almost Good Samaritan concern for the needy among them. Although, like most hippies, they seem to live without visible means of support, they manage to provide food and shelter for others.

Recently the Diggers opened a Free Store on Tenth Street near First Avenue. Here, believe it or not, everything is free; the hippies bring in things they don't need and search through the boots and clothes for something that fits. The Free Store's doorstep is decorated with inlaid pennies. The Diggers give away food, too, and have plans for a free medical clinic.

But the Diggers take drugs. Recently Orky himself took a walk on the ledge around the top of the eight-story building where he lives. He was high on LSD at the time. Luckier than many LSD-takers, he survived the trip.

Many of the buildings in Greenwich Village serve as bulletin boards for all kinds of messages. I saw this one taped to the window of an art shop:

Wanted: Someone (preferably female) to share 3-room apartment. $22. Call Steve, QU 9-2380.

Here are some more announcements I saw in the Village recently:

Has anyone seen Joe Wilson? If you see him, please ask him to call me. He has all my clothes! Alice Mason, 115-8347.

For sale: Plane ticket to San Francisco. Right price. ZE 3-9851.

Driving to Chicago Saturday. Room for two more. If you want a ride ask for Vike at Bill's Loveteria.

Mary: We don't know where you are, but your Daddy and I want you to know we love you. The police are looking for you. Please, please come home soon. You mean more to us than you know. With all our love, Mom and Dad.

All over the world, young people are running away from home and joining an international "freakout" on life. Of course, such rebellion is nothing new. Every generation must make the transition from babyhood to independence; and I imagine that at some time in his life every red-blooded boy runs away from home.

I did, when I was ten years old. Dad and Mother had the oldfashioned idea that teaching children to do something useful was a good idea, and one of my own tasks was washing and drying the supper dishes. This was a job I did not like at all, especially when some of my friends found out that the Preacher's Kid did the dishes regularly! That did it. I packed two peanut-butter sandwiches and started out into the world. I was going to make it on my own! I told myself I wasn't coming back until Dad and Mother were sorry they had made me work so hard—especially at such a sissy job as dishwashing!

When both sandwiches were gone I got hungry. I stuck it out for one whole day before returning home.

It may be amusing when a child runs away from home, because usually, as I did, he soon returns. It is not very amusing when thousands of teen-agers leave home and don't return. There is such a trend in this direction that I predict more than six hundred thousand young people will run away from home within the next few years. And most of them will be exposed to dangers that never before existed.

These are the spectacular runaways. But what of the millions of others no one knows about? Every young person who is bored, rebellious, or disillusioned is part of the new runaway generation, even if he never leaves home or grows long hair. Today's young generation is questioning everything our civilization rests on, and seems ready to follow any Pied Piper who comes along promising a new kind of trip to nowhere.

Like Skinny Carlos.

Strung Out 69

with me to the Teen Challenge Center in Brooklyn,
although he was obviously terrified.

7

Strung Out

Skinny Carlos was seventeen years old and weighed
just over a hundred pounds when I first found him at
his "home"—a urine-soaked mattress covered with
rags in a corner of a filthy basement on 110th Street in
Spanish Harlem. His parents had gone back to Puerto
Rico and left him alone in the streets, and for three
years he had been stoking the fires of the tenement
house furnace in exchange for his rat-hole sleeping
corner. Besides the dirty clothes on his emaciated
body, he owned exactly three things: a bedside calen-
dar three years old, a picture of his mother, and a
candle.

He was obviously diseased and undernourished,
and my question as to what he ate was answered with
an expressive shrug of his thin shoulders. "Sometimes
my *amigos* put me up for a meal. Other times I go to
the corner grocery and swipe oranges or bread. I bum
food wherever I can get it."

One look told me that he didn't get it very often.
I've grown pretty used to sickening situations as I
carry on my ministry around the city, but Skinny's
set-up moved me deeply. I persuaded Skinny to come

with me to the Teen Challenge Center in Brooklyn, although he was obviously reluctant.

As we left the FDR Drive to swing onto the Brooklyn Bridge, Skinny darted nervous eyes at the great structure. "What's that?" he demanded.

"The Brooklyn Bridge."

It was hard for me to believe that Skinny had not seen it before. He had never before been outside the area of eighteen to twenty blocks that was his home "turf."

The contrast between Skinny's basement and the sleek high-rise apartments we were passing struck me forcibly; I thought, as I often have, how incredible it was that in an affluent society like ours there are young people like Carlos who have no homes except basements, rooftops and subway benches. Incredible, except that I come across them so often.

When we reached the white doorway of our boys' home at 416 Clinton Avenue, Brooklyn, it was obvious that Skinny was uneasy. But it gave me great satisfaction to see him sit with the other boys at the dinner table and eat a real square meal. One of our workers took him upstairs for a shower—it was the first time he had bathed in months—and provided him with change of clothes.

The paper work involved in the administration of Teen Challenge Center and other projects is enormous and increasing all the time. Frequently, after a day spent in the streets among the boys, I come home to face long hours at my office desk. Tonight was one of those nights. The work seemed lightened by knowing that just down the hall Skinny at least was sleeping—in a real bed between two clean sheets.

By two o'clock in the morning I was just finishing up my work when I heard a blood-chilling scream. I rushed to the hall, just in time to see Skinny disappear down the long stairway and out the door. He was barefoot and half dressed. I ran after him and into the street, followed by a few others who were also awake. We could see the white glow of the shirt he clutched like a banner in the dark, but he vanished into some side street before we could catch him. For the rest of the night his parting scream rang in my ears:

"Let me outa here—I can't take it!"

I knew from experience that such boys usually return to the familiarity of their own home turf, so in the morning I set out for Spanish Harlem. About eleven o'clock I found Skinny, in a little coffee shop less than two blocks from his basement hole. He showed his embarrassment when I walked in, but he didn't evade my question. He told me what I should have realized before—the reason for his reluctance to enter Teen Challenge. In taking him away from his turf, I had taken away his security, because Skinny was a junkie.

"I can't take it without my shots," he told me bluntly. "As long as I live, man, I gotta live like a junkie, and I'll die a junkie."

I tried to persuade Skinny that others like him had made it back to the real world through the help of Teen Challenge, but he could not believe it, and he would not return. I had to leave without him, my heart heavy.

Skinny was an accurate prophet. Within a year he died in a city hospital of cirrhosis of the liver.

Skinny was "strung out," as street language puts it

—hooked on heroin, and on a way of life that left him helpless and hopeless. Many heroin addicts develop hepatitis. Skinny's autopsy showed that he had that, too. In the world where I work, the wages of sin is always death.

Fernandez paid the price on a Bronx roof top where he and five teen-age friends were "shooting it up" with heroin. Fernandez got an overdose. When that happens, fellow junkies try to revive the victim by slapping his face with a wet towel, pouring liquid down his throat, or injecting salt water into his veins. This time none of the methods worked. Terrified, the other five boys fled.

The next day all five were walking the Bronx streets together, sick and jittery and in need of another "fix." None of them had been able to get together enough money for a deck of heroin. Then one of the boys got an idea. They climbed back up the fire escape to the roof top where they'd held their party the night before. Often in an area like that, a corpse is not discovered for several days. Sure enough, their friend Fernandez was still lying where they had left him.

Between them, they managed to strip the cold, stiff body of pants, belt, shirt, shoes and socks. They left the naked corpse on the roof and ran to the nearest pawnshop, where they traded their buddy's clothes for enough cash for one bag of heroin.

Some friends, you say? But that's what a narcotic does to its victims—it can grip them so tight that they will stop at nothing on earth to get the next dose.

Taking forbidden drugs is becoming more and more common today—not only in hippie communities like Greenwich Village, but in small towns and communities all over the country. The drug scene has affected our whole culture. If you don't believe me, look in any magazine or store window, or listen to records or the radio. Music has developed "acid rock." Fashions for all ages and sizes appear in psychedelic colors. Art and advertising have taken on the overtones of an LSD trip. As a result of experiments with everything from marijuana and morning glory seeds to heroin, LSD and STP, terrible tragedies are trapping multitudes of young people today. Every year thousands of them, seeking new experiences, are dragged into a way of life that is actually hell on earth.

For the first time in history, it is possible to permanently damage your mind, your body, and your unborn children by taking a chemical you may not even know is there.

Until recent years, the problem of drug addiction was concentrated among Negro, Chinese and Puerto Rican ethnic groups in a very few of our cities. Now it has spread to college campuses, towns, and even rural areas, affecting every race and social and economic bracket across the nation. Recently the president of a PTA in Pennsylvania was arrested together with her teen-age son when a large quantity of marijuana was found in their home. A high-school principal was fired when her board of education discovered she used marijuana. The fifteen-year-old son of a district attorney was arrested on charges of selling narcotics when police found barbituates, pep pills, heroin, and a hypodermic needle in his pockets.

Apparently few young people who try to "turn on" with drugs know or care about their involvement with the underworld. Half of all the crime in New York

City is connected in some way with the sale and use of narcotics. The narcotics business is the underworld's second most lucrative racket, and the profits are constantly climbing.

Heroin is a harmless-looking white powder whose victims find its hold practically impossible to break. And the cost of a dose is not reasonable, any way you look at it. It starts with five dollars, but may soon climb to four, six or even ten times that amount per day.

"Horse," which comes, like morphine, from the opium poppy of Asia, gives its users a feeling of intense pleasure and superiority. This elated feeling is soon followed by one of strong depression. Addicts crave a daily ride on the white horse so much that they will do anything to get it—become thieves, burglars, prostitutes.

Every new victim feels a strange need to find or create new addicts for companionship. Thus heroin addiction is a vast spider web constantly expanding to capture new victims.

A heroin injection may be fatal. Early in 1967, Soupy Hirt and his pal Andrew Jones cooked up a heroin dose for Wirt's girl friend, eighteen-year-old Penelope McCall. Soupy filled a hypodermic syringe with the hot mixture and plunged it into a vein in Penelope's arm. Soon afterwards the two fell asleep in Soupy's Manhattan apartment. Two weeks later police found her body in the trunk of Soupy's rented car.

Violence and sudden death are constant companions of the heroin pushers. Teen Challenge workers have occasionally observed the kind of purchase that took place on a cold January night in Spanish Harlem.

John Espertaro bought three bags of heroin that night from a dope pusher in a dingy tenement hallway. He had made similar purchases many times. He pocketed the heroin and the pusher pocketed the money. At that point John put his companion under arrest, for John Espertaro was an undercover agent with the narcotics bureau of New York City's police department.

While John was making the arrest, four armed thugs suddenly made their appearance and jumped him. One jabbed a knife into John's stomach, one held an automatic pistol against his ear, and the other two emptied his pockets.

Undercover agents carry little cash except for bureau funds to use purchasing narcotics for evidence in cases. When the thugs found only the few dollars left in Espertaro's wallet, they became enraged and slammed his head against the floor. John screamed, "Help!"

The gunman with the pistol aimed it again at Espertaro's head, shouting, "This is for you, Baby!"

John Espertaro yanked his service revolver from under his coat and fired. His first shot went through the gunman's eye and exploded in his brain. The second went through the heart of the knifer. Nearby apartment dwellers began to scream. The other two thieves disappeared into the street.

It was a typical night in the heroin business.

Drug addicts describe mainlining heroin—injecting it directly into the veins—as "the end of the line." When anyone reaches the point where he has to mainline regularly, he's had it. There's no place left for him to go. And too often, the next step is the grave. I have no words to describe the feelings of terror and tragedy that overwhelm me when I stand before the casket of a boy like Skinny Carlos or Fernandez—boys who were once bright young teen-agers . . . who ended up strung out on "stuff."

These kids die of OD (overdose), they commit suicide, they are murdered, or they are left to die in hospitals and vacant tenements. Penelope McCall has been buried in a lonely grave along with thousands of other youngsters who got strung out. These are the twentieth-century lepers. They are the untouchables. They have strung themselves out so far and so tight that they have reached a point of no return.

A young heroin addict used to joke about Junkie Heaven, where everyone could get all the "stuff" he craved. But there is no Junkie Heaven anywhere. All the way, it's all hell.

8

Legalize Marijuana?

Nine Brooklyn boys were playing one of their favorite games with a public transit bus. When the green and white bus swung onto Dean Street and stopped at their corner, the boys acted as though they didn't even see it. But as it started down narrow Dean Street, they came to life. Jumping for the open rear windows, they hung from them while the bus careened down the street. They were all set for an exciting free ride.

At one point the bus had to thread its way between a double-parked car and truck. Benny jumped off, screaming to the others to follow suit. They didn't—until the truck wiped them off the bus "like butter," as one sickened bystander described it. Two of them died soon after they reached the hospital.

I've seen a good many similar would-be joy rides end in deep trouble. And everything I say here is written in the hope that it will come through better than the warning of Benny, who deserted that bus in time to survive. Like Benny, I know what may happen when young people begin certain trips.

Late in 1967 one of the largest caches of marijuana ever found was picked up by federal agents just outside New York City. The packets were wrapped in red, white and blue paper, and had been brought by station wagon from the Mexican border. There was enough marijuana in that one load to make more than a million cigarettes.

There is quite a campaign today to lift all the bars and to make marijuana as easy to get as aspirin. I've been appearing on radio and television panels with many so-called experts who keep talking about how harmless marijuana is and who claim that young people ought to be permitted to smoke it "to get it out of their system." On one such program, a physician was asked if he ever tried smoking marijuana to gain a more sympathetic understanding of the problems facing young people. "No!" the doctor answered with profanity, "I take it to get stoned."

Marijuana is now defintely the favorite campus drug. One student said recently, "When you went to a frat party last year they offered you a drink. This year they give you pot." At some of our largest colleges and universities, a third of the students have tried smoking "pot" or "grass" or "tea." Recently I addressed hundreds of students at a university in Mexico City. I was startled by their response to a statement I made concerning the trend in the United States toward legalizing marijuana. More than a third of the students applauded enthusiastically—indicating their wholehearted approval of such legalization.

Last fall John Steinbeck IV was roundly criticized for reporting that at least three-fourths of the servicemen in Vietnam smoke marijuana. But soon afterward Brigadier Genral Harley Moore, Jr., of Honolulu said that marijuana was a problem throughout Vietnam, and that marijuana had been found even on sentries and military policemen. He added that more servicemen in Vietnam are arrested for smoking marijuana than for any other single major offense. When the general was asked whether the men were smoking marijuana under combat conditions, he replied, "It wouldn't surprise me in the least."

In some American communities it is reported that half the young people are experimenting with marijuana. One national magazine suggests that ten million Americans have tried smoking it. Pot is "the thing" with the "in" crowd today. This is the Marijuana Generation.

Seventeen researchers from a famous western university recently issued a report on marijuana, basing their conclusions on interviews with a hundred marijuana-smoking young people during a period of one year. The researchers' main conclusion: Marijuana had not only failed to harm these users, but had been good for them. The smokers, they said, were keener, dressed better, and had gained more insight into human nature and more knowledge of the world than non-users. The report also suggested that marijuana had kept these young people from alcohol and harder drugs.

When I read that report in the *Los Angeles Times,* I was shocked and horrified. From these experts and others like them there is a growing hue and cry to legalize the smoking of marijuana and to remove the penalties restricting its possession and sale. I have found that some of the "impartial experts" who favor this admit smoking and enjoying marijuana themselves. Expecting an impartial opinion about marijuana from smokers of it is like expecting a convention of alcoholics to make an unbiased study of the effects of bourbon.

What are the facts? First of all, the estimates of the number of marijuana users may be inflated. Recently *Reader's Digest* published the findings of a Gallup poll which investigated the use of marijuana in 426 colleges.The poll indicated that not more than 6 percent of the students had ever tried marijuana, and that the total number of users is closer to 300,000 than to the larger numbers often estimated. Still, 67 percent of the students interviewed said they thought the use of drugs on campus would increase. And whether it be millions or hundreds of thousands, I'm not nearly so concerned about the total number of young people now smoking marijuana as I am about the steadily growing number who are developing a permissive attitude toward all drugs—including LSD, about which I am going to say more later—and who may eventually fall for the big lie that drug users are more worldly wise and more conscious of the possibilities of their personalities.

I disagree totally with the current permissive attitude toward marijuana. I *consider marijuana the most dangerous drug used today.*

I have been working with drug addicts for ten years. At Teen Challenge we have counseled two thousand of them—as many as any private agency in the world. I know what marijuana does.

Is marijuana dangerous? The answer is positively yes. Ninety-five percent of all the drug addicts we have ever treated began with marijuana and then graduated to harder stuff. We ask each of these addicts

how he got started on the road to narcotics and almost always the answer is, "I took a stick of pot." The
federal penalty for possession of marijuana is a minimum of two years in the penitentiary; the penalty for
sale or delivery of the drug is a minimum of five
years. The reasons for these stringent federal laws
against the sale and possession of marijuana were eli-
cited in a Congressional Committee report in which
345 witnesses received information from more than
2,000 doctors, hospitals, prisons and law enforcement
officers. Briefly, the findings of the committee were: 1.
That heroin and marijuana were the two most widely
used illicit drugs, with more than half of the total
crime in the largest cities of the nation being trace-
able directly or indirectly to the use of these drugs. 2.
That marijuana, though not addictive, is habit-
forming; its extended use causes psychic dependency;
habitual use, as in many instances, has led to serious
crimes and insanity. 3. That over 75 percent of the
heroin addicts interviewed began with marijuana and
graduated to more powerful drugs.

The World Health Organization in 1965 included
among the psychological and physiological effects of
marijuana smoking the following: impairment of judge-
ment and memory; illusions and delusions predis-
posing to antisocial behavior; anxiety and aggressive-
ness as a result of the various intellectual and sen-
sory derangements. A well known medical society reported after extensive studies that marijuana in its
strongest forms such as hashish is definitely associated
with violence, insanity and criminality. The government of Egypt, where habitual use of marijuana has
reportedly reached the alarming rate of 30 percent of

the population, states that this drug is capable of destroying brain cells and of inducing acts of violence—even murder, and that it is in fact a thoroughly vicious and dangerous thing and of no value whatever to humanity, and deserving of nothing but the odium and contempt of a civilized people.

Dr. Norman Maylor, a botanist, states that "continued marijuana use leads straight to the lunatic asylum." It is true that some people are so constituted that a single experience with marijuana or LSD produces no lasting effects, or none that are thus far recognizable. It is true that some marijuana smokers never go on to hard narcotics. However, the constitutions of some individuals are such that a single large dose of either marijuana or LSD has been known to result in suicide, homicide or temporary insanity.

I know what marijuana does. It breaks down resistance to other drugs. It paves the way to alcoholism and drug addiction. It destroys moral values, especially sex standards. It speeds up heart action, dilates the pupils of the eyes, and slows muscle response. It increases laziness and anti-social attitudes. It destroys inhibitions, impairs judgment, gives a person a feeling of greater capability that he actually has, and distorts his sense of time and space.

That's a perfect setup for automobile wrecks. A good many accidents today are caused by pot-smoking teen-agers careening down a highway while they listen to someone on the car radio saying that marijuana isn't harmful.

There's a substance in marijuana known as THC; it can produce illusions, delusions, and hallucinations. One pot-smoker thought he stood outside himself and watched himself shrink, die, and be buried. Enough THC will produce psychotic reactions.

The people who want to legalize marijuana base their arguments on very fuzzy theories. They want the right to use it simply because it gives them pleasure. When they are asked to answer to the fact that the unrestricted use of marijuana could be highly dangerous, they fall back on the argument that marijuana is no worse than alcohol. They seem to feel that they have a constitutional right to experiment to the limit, and for their own selfish indulgence they violate and try to overthrow carefully enacted federal laws.

There is no question in my mind that anyone who will try marijuana will try LSD. When a college kid comes to me and says he is smoking marijuana but that he doesn't intend to go on to other drugs, I know that he's not telling the truth. He has started on marijuana because he is not satisfied with life, and he will go the whole route. He'll keep making compromises all the way to the bitter end.

The first stick of pot a young person smokes is the beginning of a disease that will destroy unless it is stopped.

One of the most serious dangers from marijuana is the very fact that it's considered so harmless. "The student who cares about his health," one college student said, "smokes marijuana now. After all, no one has yet proven that it's anywhere near as harmful as liquor or cigarettes." This idea that marijuana is harmless hooks a lot of suckers. Frequently parents will bring a marijuana-smoking son or daughter to me for help—and *I can't help them*, because the smoker has gotten the idea, "I'm really not hooked, and I'll never become a junkie. Tea isn't that bad." In the time since the permissive propaganda about marijuana has spread around the country, I have not been able to help one such smoker.

The irony of it is that a year later the same youngster will come back, dirty and unshaven and hooked on heroin. That's the end of the route. I wish every expert who thinks marijuana is so great could see this as often as I do.

So when I hear that the dangers of marijuana have been over-rated, I call that statement on outright lie. Whether you call marijuana addictive or habit-forming or "habituating"—and it actually makes no difference, because the results almost always are the same dead end—its dangers are far more serious than many are ready to recognize. As far as I'm concerned, marijuana is more dangerous than LSD. Because it is considered harmless and because it is so widely accepted, marijuana leads thousands of users into deadly experiments with the drugs that bend minds and bodies until they break.

I have some advice for all teen-agers who want to be straight and strong. You can identify marijuana cigarettes because they are rolled shut at both ends, and they have a very strong sweet odor. If you know that someone is smoking or peddling pot—be a rat! Report it to the police immediately. If you think that is going too far, ask yourself just this one question: "How would I like it if someone offered that stick of pot to my younger brother or sister?"

Most important of all, let's not fall for the idea that "pot heads" and "acid heads" are really the "in" group.

Let's see them for what they are—just a lot of lost, mixed-up, sick, unstable, insecure, seedy, long-haired dropouts.

9

Blow Your Mind . . .

Five students from a western university were climbing a mountain. As they scrambled higher through the purple sagebrush, their minds seemed to soar even higher in the fantastically clear air. New sounds burst in their eardrums; colors of incredible brightness flowed all around them.

The three young men and the two young women sat down on a rocky precipice and looked into the midday sun. Never before had they realized how living and conscious a thing it was. Its rays leaped out from the purple-gold center, curled into multicolored flames, licked toward them, seeming to engulf them. Together the five students chanted a hymn of praise to their brother in space.

Suddenly, the light faded. They were again engulfed, this time in darkness—and in fear, for they knew that it was still the time of broad daylight. Sightlessly, they tried to grope their way down the

NOTE—*Early in 1968, wide publicity was given the alleged blindness of six students from a Pennsylvania university who were reported to have stared at the sun while on a similar LSD trip. The whole incident was later exposed as a hoax. The student tragedy I have reported here, however, has been carefully verified.*

steep mountain. Rescuers rushed them to a hospital where the medical staff did what it could. Fortunately, each of the students retained some perception of light. Unfortunately, none of the five will ever again have normal vision.

During the whole experience, the five had been "on a trip"—they had been under the influence of LSD.

In spite of such disasters, LSD is rapidly becoming more and more popular with young people. Uncounted thousands of college students have tried it; many high-schoolers are experimenting with it; to most hippies it is the most in thing yet. Its use—recently reported even in the armed forces—is reaching epidemic proportions.

LSD is a hallucinatory chemical compound without color or taste but so powerful that an amount the size of an aspirin tablet will affect the minds of fifteen hundred people. A reporter who swallowed a capsule of LSD in the interests of research saw exotic-colored lights flashing on and off, thought he was breathing out flowers, and saw blue sparks when he snapped his fingers. But then he felt that the music he had been listening to was solidifying and crushing him. He experienced intense pains throughout his body, and thought he was dissolving. He wrote of the experience: "I have never been more terrified in my life."

Another man who took LSD thought that he had become an orange, and locked himself in his room from fear of turning into orange juice. A student user thought he was a green plant. A woman who tried it thought she was a grease spot. A college girl believed she had disappeared after taking her third dose. A teen-ager thought buildings were falling on him. Another boy wrecked his car, a whole year after his having taken LSD, because of hallucination that a hundred headlights were converging on him.

Laurence took LSD, said he was going to bed, and jumped out his sixth-floor window. Another boy thought he could fly and jumped off a cliff. Two New York homosexuals had a fight after taking LSD, wrecked their expensive apartment, and made such a racket that neighbors called the police. When they arrived, one of the youths jumped out the window; the other had to be taken to Bellevue in a straitjacket. A girl killed her boy friend with a butcher knife and didn't even know she had done it.

Last summer several San Francisco hippies had some grim experiences with LSD. One took LSD and jumped off a dam; another took a dose and jumped in front of a train. Neither survived. Sam Russell was found dead in the Haight-Ashbury apartment he had painted in psychedelic colors. He had been stabbed many times with a butcher knife and his right forearm had been severed. Police soon picked up his "friend," Gene Murphy, who was riding around with the missing arm in his Volkswagen. Sam, it seemed, had sold Gene some LSD that gave him a bad trip, and Gene's reaction had been murder. "He was convulsing as he went down," said Gene. "That's why I stabbed him some more."

Only two years ago the New York papers screamed out the details of another case history. The bodies of a seventeen-year-old girl and her twenty-three-year-old hippie boy friend were discovered in a dingy Village basement. Police arriving to investigate walked past a gigantic painting of a nude girl and entered through a door across which were scrawled the words, *Free Love*. The corpses were naked, their heads beaten in. The two had been using marijuana and hallucinatory drugs; they had gone to an LSD party the night before and had entered the basement in search of the drug.

At the same time that police were seeking their murderers, a law student was on trial in New York City for the murder of his mother-in-law. Christopher Flint had taken a number of LSD trips. On the first one, he reported, "My chair turned to blood. The ceiling began to come down. The roof split in half. The walls began to curve." He found himself in the characteristic crouch of a catatonic trance, in a state of deep fear. During another LSD session, he mistook an automobile for a bat. On Christopher's fifth trip, his mother-in-law was murdered. He could not remember whether he had killed her.

In California, a sixteen-year-old boy was rushed to the hospital after a bad trip with LSD. There he slashed his wrists with a knife, and his life was saved by the hospital attendants just in time. The boy was next put in a room from which everything but his bed had been taken. As soon as he was left alone he gouged his eyes with his fingers. Finally he succeeded in strangling himself.

In our San Francisco Teen Challenge Center we worked with a nineteen-year-old LSD user from a good family. We thought that we were getting through to him, but two weeks later, in the middle of a chapel service, he suddenly went down on the floor on all fours and started barking like a dog. He grabbed a Bible and scratched at the pages, animal-fashion. His mind was blown completely.

LSD has already sent hundreds of users to mental institutions; it can produce everything from paranoia and delusions to schizophrenia and epileptic convulsions. It also breaks down chromosomes. A young mother who had taken LSD only once gave birth to a baby with a deformed skull and a serious intestinal defect. Doctors expect that LSD is going to produce a crop of babies with mongolism, abnormal bone structure, and other defects so horrible as to make thalidomide seem practically harmless in comparison.

The LSD movement has a prophet who goes about the country urging young people to "turn on, tune in, and drop out." Far too many of them are doing it. This would-be youth leader claims that LSD brings its users to God; for a while he set up shop in Greenwich Village, not far from our Lost Coin coffeehouse, and celebrated his own "sacrament" with LSD. He has even introduced his own daughter to this frightening drug. Her account of growing up in his psychedelic community, published recently in a national magazine, is shocking and pathetic.

I have been told by young intellectuals that LSD is harmless and helpful under controlled conditions, and that I ought to do some more research into it. I have done my research where the ivory tower intellectuals have not—in the streets. I have stood there helplessly when the LSD users were barking like dogs; I have been called in when they have blown their minds and have tried to kill themselves, and I have had to bury them when they succeeded.

To many people the letters LSD are closely associated with the name of Timothy Leary. Leary, once a professor at Harvard University, seems to think of LSD in terms of sex. According to an interview in *Playboy* magazine, Leary has said: "An LSD session that does not involve an ultimate merging with a person of the opposite sex isn't really complete."

I wish Professor Leary could hear what Kathy Johnson had to say about his favorite drug. A few months ago, just eighteen years old and two months pregnant, she was sitting in the stale air of an East Twelfth Street bar waiting for her common-law husband to return home from Rikers Island where he was doing time on a drug charge. She seemed out of place in that garish atmosphere, but I could understand why she preferred it to her third-floor apartment. I had seen the rickety furniture which she had salvaged from sidewalk refuse heaps, the stained bathtub in the kichen, the toilet that had no seat. The window above it is broken, and in winter the toilet freezes solid except for an occasional thawing out with boiling water from the filthy gas stove.

The talk in the bar shifted from sex to LSD. "Ever try it?" one of the drinkers asked Kathy.

A mirthless smile curved her lips. "You mean Lethal, Suicidal and Disastrous? That's what I think of it. If you want to talk to someone who's tried it, go to Bellevue and talk to one of the DWA's."

"Whatcha mean, DWA's?" asked another drinker. "Dontcha mean DOA, Dead on Arrival?"

"No," Kathy answered, thinking of the mindless, vegetable existence of the LSD user she knew best. "I mean DWA—Dead Without Arriving."

10

"I Was in Hell"

I work in a crazy jungle. The young people who get hooked on drugs sometimes say they have a monkey on their back—and they can't get it off. Yet what really plagues a junkie is not the physical habit, but the mind habit. The physical habit can be kicked in three or four days, cold turkey—but the mind habit sticks for life. *Unless the power of God overthrows the hold of Satan.*

One of the new drugs makes even LSD look weak. "Taking LSD," one experimenter said, "is like being let out of a cage—taking STP is like being shot out of a cannon."

STP, which may get its name from a gasoline additive ("scientifically treated petroleum"), *really* blows a mind. While a dose of LSD may last all night, STP's effects usually continue for three or four *days*. Last summer young victims began showing up in hospitals in several cities with speeded-up pulses, blurred vision, and frightening nightmares. Some of them had to be put in straitjackets.

A young woman in California swallowed three capsules of STP and got a good feeling; half an hour later she felt miserable and depressed, she thought her mind was shrinking, and then she found that her vocal cords were paralyzed. After that she stopped breathing—her *lungs* were paralyzed.

Rushed to the hospital, she was cared for until she could enter a mental institution. The last time I heard of her, she was still there. This is how she described what STP did to her: "I saw myself on fire and then I began to feel the pain of fire. If I closed my eyes I knew I would die . . . *I was in hell.*"

More than 5,000 capsules of STP were distributed at one party in the San Francisco area. A man who has been credited with supplying young people with both LSD and STP says the latter stands for serenity, tranquility and peace. Apparently some people believe him.

After the couple mentioned in the preceding chaper were found murdered in Greenwich Village, some of their friends said that both of them had previously taken "speed." By which they meant the two had been taking a drug—methedrine—which is coming into increasing use in Greenwich Village and Haight-Ashbury.

One hippy said recently of methedrine, "You get a really strong sex urge. You get a fantastic rush—a feeling that you're speeded up, you can do anything." The "freaks" inject it directly into their veins, and when they do this every two hours, they get a high that may last a week.

Methedrine is one kind of pep pill. Last summer a famous rock 'n roll singer was given a prison sentence for possession of pep pills. A lot of young people take pep pills for extra energy and a feeling that everything is wonderful (sometimes with hallucinations).

A truck driver who had taken a number of these pills —probably to keep alert—charged along a fog-drenched turnpike at nearly 70 miles an hour. His truck struck another one, which produced a chain reaction involving a total of three automobiles, twelve trucks, and six deaths. What happened is what often happens with drugs; they may affect the mind and body in unexpected ways. Pep pills can produce mental delusions and warp the judgment. And in today's high-speed world, it's important to be *really* alert— not to have the delusion of alertness alongside distorted reactions.

That extra energy, of course, doesn't spring out of thin air. What amphetamines—the stimulants pep pills are usually made of—actually do is to postpone natural fatigue. But old Mother Nature won't be short-changed. Sooner or later the body pays the bill; for example, when a user quits taking the pills, he has to get back some of the sleep he lost while he was riding high. And that good feeling he had is followed by one of pessimism and depression. Everything evens out in the end.

Another thing about pep pills is also true of many other drugs. The more you take, the more you need; each time you try them, you need a few more to get the same effect. A medical student—who should have known better—was taking dozens of pep pills a day to get through a stiff series of examinations when Mother Nature caught up with him. He fell asleep in the middle of his hardest exam, and had the good sense to learn his lesson. He put a stop to a very dangerous habit.

The amphetamine compounds can be put to good

use by a physician, but—like any poison—in the hands of an amateur, they can do incredible damage.

Some of the hippies are getting wise to the amphetamine they call "speed." One of them said recently, "That stuff's no good, man—it makes your mind like Swiss cheese." And a new kind of button is beginning to appear in the Village. It reads: "SPEED KILLS."

Last summer the manager of a world-famous singing group died after a party—apparently from an overdose of barbiturates. Not long ago twenty-two teen-agers in Queens were found guilty of possession of four kinds of drugs, including LSD, marijuana, and barbiturates. More than 3,000 Americans die every year from barbiturates; no other drug kills as many.

Barbiturates are the opposite of amphetamines—they are taken for relaxation and sleep. The main ingredient in a good many sleeping pills and sedatives, "barbies" are often known by such exotic names as Blue Heavens, Yellowjackets, Red Birds, and Purple Hearts.

Nearly a thousand different companies make barbiturates—by the billions. Tragically, many fall into the hands of crooks and scoundrels who pass them on to addicts and abusers. And while sedatives of this type can be very useful, the barbiturates are so abused that they are among the most dangerous drugs made.

Barbiturates are habit-forming, and the habit is often harder and more dangerous to "kick" than heroin addiction. Overdoses lead to depression, nausea, incoherency, and death.

There seems to be no end to the ways young people will try to get high. Several years ago I was among the first to warn against the dangers of a fad that be-

came popular among high-schoolers for some time—
glue sniffing. This can and does kill. A number of
teen-age boys and girls in Bradenton, Florida, were
discovered smoking the dried leaves of the periwinkle
plant. It gave them the feeling that ants were crawling over them, and other hallucinations. What they
didn't know was that periwinkle could destroy their
white blood cells, their hair and their muscle tissue.

I have often asked myself why so many young people today are experimenting with so many dangerous
products. One day I found the answer in the last book
of the Bible. This is what I read: "Woe to the inha-
biters of the earth . . . for the devil is come down unto
you, having great wrath, because he knoweth that he
hath but a short time" (Revelation 12:12).

There is a demonic power at work in the world
today, seeking to enslave and destroy everyone possible—especially young people—by using everything
available to corrupt and kill, trying to distort the
minds of young people for all kinds of evil purposes.
Now, that demonic power cannot touch a well-adjusted
mind. I think it's ironic and symbolic that LSD is
called a "mind-bender."

Throughout Bible history there is evidence that demonic possession is shown by the possessed one's way
of dressing. The psychedelic colors and fashions of
today are an expression of this; people are trying to
live out, consciously or unconsciously, way-out visions
and hallucinations. Dress and art try to capture the
exotic experiences of trips and drugs.

Drug addiction and the bohemian way of life are
now spreading around the world. And these form a
new religion for many of the hippies. The only route

they know to a feeling of well-being, security and pleasure is through drugs.

They take these drugs for the "kicks" and the weird visions they get from them. Now, *visions* are the legitimate experience of young people. The prophet Joel prophesied that God would pour out His Spirit upon all flesh, and that at that time, "your old men shall dream dreams, your young men shall see visions" (2:28). Those who seek visions through synthetic drugs are trying to capture *an experience they should have*—but by using drugs they bypass the true religious experience.

I am a young man, and I have seen visions. Visions of the glory and beauty of Jesus Christ, and of His wonderful revelations; visions of what Christ is ready to do for this generation. He offers the experiences that can give the greatest thrills of all without risking the destruction of mind, body and soul.

11

"Stamp Out Virginity!"

No one seems to know how or why it started, but one Labor Day week end in the quiet community of Hampton Beach, New Hampshire, a senseless riot erupted. More than ten thousand high-school and college students had swarmed into Hampton Beach for one last fling before going back to school—and suddenly they went berserk. They hurled rocks and bricks, smashed windowns, looted and burned stores, and assaulted bystanders. The National Guard had to be called in before order could be restored.

A police officer who was on the scene told me: "It was indescribable. Nothing could stop those kids; a wicked spirit seemed to get inside them and spread destruction like wildfire over the whole beach and town. It was as if they were possessed by some insane entity from another world."

A year later a number of Christian workers walked with me through the same area, witnessing to thousands of students who had returned for another fling. I saw a well-tanned college boy carrying a case of beer down the beach, and I asked him why he was there.

"Mister," he said, "there's only one reason. The fellows cruise the streets and beaches looking for girls, and you might be surprised how many of those chicks in bikinis are here looking for boys. We have a ball!"

As he went down the beach and set down the beer in the middle of a ring of young fellows and girls, I made out the words on one of their beach towels: "STAMP OUT VIRGINITY."

The police in various parts of the country tell me that the beach and resort areas are especially plagued by three problems, each rapidly increasing: crime, drugs, and venereal disease. The No. 1 teen-age problem in Miami is pregnancy. In the United States, one girl in five is pregnant at her wedding. Illegitimate births among teen-agers doubled in the last twenty-five years—and increased *four* times among women twenty to twenty-five. More than a quarter of a million fatherless babies are born each year in this country, and there are more than a million abortions.

A girl in a cultured suburban community said that going to a drive-in movie was practically an invitation to intercourse. In 1929 two-thirds of the girls in college and half the college men had never engaged in pre-marital sex. Today this is true of only half of the girls and only a third of the men. Our country is faced with an explosive increase in adultery, divorce, venereal disease, and mental problems created by illicit sex.

There is probably too much loose talk about "the sex revolution" today, yet there is no question that the revolution is real. Late last summer a teen-age girl was raped in Central Park after her companion was nearly killed. He was a man she had "married" in a flower ceremony, the girl said, and she was living with him. She did not know his real name. Sex without limitations is one of the demands of the hippie rebellion, but in this as in many other things the hippies simply bring to a focus the attitudes of a whole lot of young people.

I wish those who think I shouldn't speak so frankly about sex could see some of the frightened young people who turn to Teen Challenge for help. A letter of confession came to me from a teen-age girl who signed her name "Rebel." The letter I wrote her was returned to me unopened. On the outside of the envelope this note was scrawled. *"Rebel is no longer with us. She took her life."*

As I went backstage after a youth crusade in a midwestern theater, I was stopped short by a lovely teen-age girl. She was weeping like a lost child. "Reverend Wilkerson," she sobbed, "what can I do? I've just been to the doctor, and there's no way out. I'm going to have a baby for sure. Why did I do it? What do I do now? How do I tell my Mom? Where can I go?"

I gave this girl the best counsel I could, but I have often thought of her since. Many people are very permissive about sex today, but I know how explosive it is—how easily it can blow a young life to bits. The teen-age suicide rate is shooting up like a rocket, and I think I know the main reasons. In a great many cases, frightened young people have been trapped by the results of illicit sex and see no way out. They are afraid to face their parents, their friends, or the consequences. Their way out is to take their own lives.

I wish you could see some of the letters I've received, like this one from fourteen-year-old Karen:

Dear Rev. Wilkerson:

My Mom and Dad just found out I'm pregnant. I just don't know what to do now. They can't believe it—every time they look at me, Dad glowers and Mom just starts crying. She keeps saying, "It's not true, Honey. Wait and see—it will turn out all right."

But they just don't understand. I know it *is* true, and I wish I knew what to do. I'm so sad and sick I feel like killing myself. It sure wasn't worth all I've been through. And my boy friend hates me now. What's the use of living?

Can you find a home for the baby, Rev. Wilkerson? Will you tell me what to do? Please, please help me. I'm desperate!

Karen

These are the hurts I think about when I remember Hampton Beach, or when someone asks, "Why shouldn't sex be the private business of the people involved?"

I can't forget something else about Hampton Beach. Before I left there I saw once more the boy who had been carrying the case of beer. I asked him this question:

"Are you satisfied with what you're doing here? You said you're having a ball. Honestly now, are you, really?"

That handsome college student looked jolted—and

ashamed. "Mr. Wilkerson," he said, "the truth is that I'm not. I don't think there's one fellow or girl at Hampton who's really happy. Sex is an escape. We're looking for something that satisfies, even for a few minutes, but I don't think anyone here has found it yet. The whole world is so phony! So we just stop and get off for a little while when we get the chance."

Julie Conover was quite different from the Hampton Beach crowd. She was just sixteen when she went on her first date with Tom Parely. Julie's father was a minister in West Virginia, and before she would go out with Tom, Julie brought him to the parsonage for dinner.

You should have seen this perfect gentleman pull his car up the Conover driveway at ten miles an hour, as slow as a snail; he knew better than to honk the horn. When he came to the door he presented a big bouquet to Julie's mother. He politely complimented Mr. Conover on his last sermon (Tom had started attending Julie's church) and he displayed table manners that were perfect.

Julie smiled in appreciation while Tom got her father talking about politics, morals, the church youth program. The whole family nodded approval when he topped it all off by helping with the dishes. How could Julie's parents refuse when Tom asked to take her for a ride?

"No, sir," the minister must have thought, watching Tom's car pull slowly out of the driveway, "that Tom's no hot-rodder—he's a gentleman if ever there was one!"

Two blocks later—*zoom*—the car was doing thirty

. . . forty . . . fifty . . . seventy miles an hour "Here we go, Baby—Speedsville!"

Julie wasn't really surprised at all. She knew what Tom was like. She had heard the kids whisper about his fast reputation. Julie also knew what Tom was up to when he parked the car on a lonely road near Henley's Dam. When he kissed her, she acted as if it was nothing. And one thing led to another, as it usually does. Julie thought at first, *I'll let him go so far and no further*. But she came to a point of no return, and before she knew what was happening, it was too late.

After that, something happened that often does after illicit sex takes place. Tom never tried to date Julie again. Instead, he spread untrue stories about her in school. And for a long time, Julie would remember how Tom had looked into her eyes and murmured, "I love you, Julie"—and she would clench her hands and sob.

Some girls in a home for unwed mothers were asked if they had any advice for other girls. One of them said emphatically, "I advise them to stay virgins."

Another girl answered the interviewer: "The trouble is, the boy usually says, 'If you really love me, you'll make me happy.' When a boy tells a girl that, she should just say, 'If you really love me, you won't ask me to do something I shouldn't.' "

Being "in love" seems to justify any form of sex, these days. An officer in an Illinois church left his wife for a young widow in the choir. When the pastor talked with him about it, his defense was: "I love her, and I don't love my wife any more."

What is love? The fact is that love is a catch-all word which means quite a number of different things, some of them contradictory—as the unwed mother in that home realized. At one time or another, all of us experience various kinds of love—for our parents, for family, for pets, for country, for friends, and for someone of the opposite sex.

The business of being "in love" needs a little examination. A giddy feeling about someone isn't necessarily a good foundation for a lifetime with that person. I have been studying sex and marriage in many parts of the world, and I have found that in many countries and in most cultures through the ages, marriage is not based at all on what we call romantic love. Yet a surprising number of these marriages have been successful.

I'm not surprised that there's so much confusion about love and sex today. Movies, books, magazine advertisements, and radio and television commercials constantly try to put across the idea that two people are likely to fall "in love" for no better reason than that he shaves with Smoothe cream, or she dyes her hair with Lady Blonde, or he drives a Wildcat convertible. Then one or the other falls out of love, and into love with someone else when that someone comes along with a new sex-appealing product.

You won't even find guidance where you might expect it. The chaplain at a girls' school told them that "sex is fun" and that premarital sex "can be very beautiful." He added: "There are no laws about sex . . . absolutely no laws."

In 1962 a famous university permitted its male students to bring girls into their rooms for three hours every other Sunday afternoon. Newspaper reporters showed up at the dormitories that first Sunday, and one reporter asked a girl who was entering with her date whether her father knew she was there. She said, "I hope not!" At that time the university decreed that doors must be left open on these occasions "the width of a book." The students chose paperbacks and matchbooks to gauge the width.

In 1963 the same university extended its "parietal hours," as these dating-in-bedroom periods were called, to nine p.m. on Friday and to midnight on Saturday. The next year they extended further, on student demand, to midnight Friday and an hour later on Saturday. And requirements for keeping the doors open even a book-width were dropped. In 1965 the university ended its previous prohibition against alcohol in the dormitories.

A number of colleges took similar action, and today it is possible for college boys and girls to spend a great deal of time together in one another's rooms. At one famous university where daily visits are permitted, a student may have a girl friend in his room sixty-two hours a week. Another Ivy League school has eighty-four visiting hours weekly. During such visits it is often the custom for the boy to hang his necktie on the doorknob as a way of saying, "Do not disturb."

When one young mother went back to her alma mater for an alumni weekend, she found her old dormitory full of girls, boys, and beer. And she vowed that the children she had been planning to send there would get their education somewhere else.

Not all parents are so disturbed by the new developments. In fact, the colleges with the new parietal hours claim that they have simply yielded to the way things are nowadays at high school and home. When one father brought his freshman daughter into a dormitory that housed both girls and men at opposite ends of the building, he asked with apparent nonchalance, "Does coeducational housing mean every other room?"

Nevertheless, probably few parents let their adolescent children entertain their friends of the opposite sex in their bedrooms. And as psychoanalyst Carl Binger has commented, "If (the college authorities) permit girls to go to boys' rooms and remain there until late, then they should realize what the consequences are likely to be." The actual consequences are indicated by these titles of articles taken from a single issue of a professional journal for women deans and college counselors:

"College Youth and Sexual Confusion."
"Premarital Sex Norms in America and Scandinavia."
"The Variety and Meaning of Premarital Heterosexual Experiences for the College Student."
"Premarital Pregnancies and Their Outcome."

The results apparently surprised some of the college authorities. Harvard officials, according to Dean John Monro, were "badly shaken up . . . by some severe violations of decent standards of behavior." When asked what violations he meant, he said that some students were indulging in "wild parties and sexual intercourse." Harvard psychiatrist Graham B.

Blaine, Jr., wrote in the *New York Times:* "The logic of combining sex with love rather than isolating it in an otherwise casual and meaningless relationship seems valid and appealing at first blush; but looked at in the light of the increasing number of unwanted pregnancies and hasty, ill-advised marriages, it seems far less attractive."

Many oldsters seem to assume that "nice" young people never think of actually engaging in sexual intercourse, and thousands of young people do still maintain Christian standards of morality. Still, the trend today is definitely away from the old standards. A survey of the seniors at one college revealed that 13 percent do not believe in premarital intercourse—while an overwhelming 83 percent *do*. And while many students insist that most premarital sex is "monogamous"—at least at the time—the attractive coed who admitted going to bed with some boys "just to see what would happen" speaks for at least one segment of the student world.

College sex has put some new meanings into old words. "Monogamous" means "sleeping only with a girl with whom you have established a meaningful relationship"; "promiscuous" means "sleeping around with several different dates within a short period of time."

Many people have worried that the parietal rules have encouraged illicit sex. Some seem to feel that this is exactly what a college should do. A psychologist at one university said that the main question with sex is not whether it is right or wrong but whether it will "enhance individuals." Calling the students at his university immature because so few took advantage of the visiting hours in the bedrooms, he said: "I felt that this was in part a reflection of the fact that a number of students are not very eager and ready for heterosexual experience." And a group of psychiatrists who surveyed sex on various campuses called upon the colleges to adopt two sets of principles regarding sexual conduct: one set for "the student who finds rules useful as a protection or limit" and one for "the more mature student whose development will require some elbow room for experimentation."

One result of all this experimentation, in addition to the increase in hasty marriages, venereal disease, pregnancies, and abortions, is psychological. In the May, 1967 *Journal of the American Medical Association,* psychiatrist Seymour L. Halleck said that a significant number of students are "casualties of the sexual revolution." Noting the increase in emotional problems revolving around sexual choices, he said that 86 percent of the women who were psychiatric patients at the Universtiy of Wisconsin had engaged in intercourse—four times the proportion among the other women students. He concluded: "Permissive sexual activity seems to be highly correlated with mental illness."

A lot of doctors and psychiatrists knew that already. And a lot of non-specialists have known for a long time that things even out. As I said before, you can't trick Mother Nature. Or God.

Sex is one of the most wonderful, exciting, beautiful, and powerful forces in the world. God Himself designed this force; but like anything powerful, it can be used for great good, or abused to produce great harm. I've seen too many examples of the human wreckage its abuse can create to go along with the propagandists for a sex philosophy of "anything goes."

Sigmund Freud is often quoted by these propagandists for their own purposes. Let me quote what he had to say in his book *New Introductory Lectures on Psychoanalysis* about gratification of the sexual impulse:

"We believe that civilization has been built up by sacrifices in gratification of the primitive impulses, and that it is to a great extent forever being re-created as each individual repeats the sacrifice of his instinctual pleasures for the common good. The sexual are amongst the most important of the instinctual forces thus utilized: they are in this way sublimated, that is to say, their energy is turned aside from its sexual goal and diverted towards other ends, no longer sexual and socially more valuable."

Many wise men and women are fearful that our civilization, slowly erected over the centuries, will crumble as Freud intimated it might if sex is not sublimated, but allowed to gain the upper hand. Surely everyone who loves his country and appreciates the values of our culture will seek to hold the dikes against today's flood of irresponsibility, insubordination and immorality.

Let me go back to that chaplain, who should have known better, who said "There are no laws about sex." I have to disagree one hundred percent. There are laws of God sometimes known as the Ten Commandments, and there is a law that says, "Thou shalt not commit adultery." In I Corinthians 6:18 the Bible says, "Flee fornication." That covers any kind of sex outside of marriage.

Sex is so important and beautiful that God protects it inside the marriage relationship. Outside marriage, sex is wrong. It's as simple as that. So God safeguards the family, the home, and the nation. No giddy feeling about being in love can change any of this, any more than jumping off the Empire State Building can change the law of gravity.

If you have never taken part in wrong sex activities, thank God and stay clean. You'll never be proud of wallowing in the dirt. Make this your prayer: "Create in me a clean heart, O God; and renew a right spirit within me" (Psalm 51:10).

If you have been fooling around with sex in ways that you know are wrong, stop while there is time. Let God lead you into a life that really satisfies!

One thing more: Normal young men want to marry virgins. As one boy put it, "When you're just hot-rodding around, any old jalopy will do—but when you grow up and want to show some class, you want a new car."

I'll admit that I'm an old-fashioned square in the eyes of some people. I still believe in virginity. Young fellow or girl, be a square too—it's more exciting!

12

Phonies

"The hippies are more honest with themselves than anyone else is," said a San Francisco cab driver. Whether or not you buy that opinion, you'll probably agree that no one is quicker than young people at spotting phonies and fakes. This is an area where I feel a great deal of sympathy with today's teen-age rebels. Their rebellion feeds on their disenchantment with *a society that lives a lie*.

One weekend when the fleet was in the New York harbor, I met two young sailors with shawls over their shoulders, beads around their necks, and bracelets with little bells on their wrists and ankles. For all the world they reminded me of demented Oriental monks. Since they were willing to talk, I soon learned that both of them came from western states. One was from a small town in Idaho, and his parents were church members. Yet on weekends and leaves, he and his buddy put on this weird garb and lived with other hippies. I kept wondering why.

"I'll tell you," said the young sailor. "My mom and dad used to go to church and work in community affairs, but it was all a fake. They were really the opposite of all that—they didn't care how they acted in

111

private, as long as they looked respectable. That's all that counted with either of them.

"They tried to sell me that kind of life, and it just made me sick. My hippie friends may not be respectable, but at least they're honest. If they're bums, they're honest bums."

In Greenwich Village I often see one young girl whose skirt is so short you wouldn't believe it. I know her father, a highly respected minister. One day this girl came to me with a strange confession. "My dad knows how I dress and the kind of friends I run around with. Sometimes I think he's going to bawl me out, but every time he chickens out. I can't handle it—he's too easygoing and I'm paying the price. *Why doesn't my father try to do something to keep me from going to hell?*"

The most heartbreaking aspect of all my work is the great number of teen-agers who come to me brokenhearted and beg for my prayers. Over and over I hear them say things like this:

"Please pray for my dad and mom; they are getting a divorce. I don't want my home to break up. Dad and Mom fight all the time; they don't love each other, but I love them both and I still need them. If all you say about God is true, Mr. Wilkerson, please ask Him to keep our family from breaking up."

Sometimes, after meetings when I have heard dozens of such pitiful pleas, I have had to bow my head and cry in shame. Even though I believe in miracles, there are no magic formulas in my prayer. Deep in my heart I know that unless certain mothers and fathers wake up soon, there will be many teen-agers who will hold terrible thoughts of bitterness and hatred toward them for walking out.

We live in a phony age. Businessmen talk about integrity and cheat their customers. Labor leaders talk about fair play and practice racial discrimination. Government leaders mouth words about peace while they make war, and in the name of freedom and truth lie to their own citizens and imprison others.

We Americans talk a lot about freedom, and justice for all, but after nearly two centuries we seem to be just beginning to treat everyone with equal fairness. While we preached freedom to the world, we supplied arms to the French to hold down Algeria, overlooked the tyranny of Chiang Kai-shek in China, and supported the dictatorship of Batista in Cuba.

From my contacts with thousands of ministers and Christian workers, I know how deeply dedicated most of them are. But a clerical collar isn't a halo. A New England minister beat his wife unconscious and left her locked in their apartment with the gas range turned on. He then drove to another state with a member of his former choir, married her, and became pastor of another church. The minister's wife recovered enough to turn off the gas and seek help, and as a result this clergyman faces serious legal charges.

A few weeks ago a pastor came to see me at an altar service in a midwestern city. He was weeping as he talked, and it took some time to learn his problem. He began:

"Brother Wilkerson, I have just come through a nervous breakdown. And the reason is you."

"I'm sorry to hear that," I said, completely taken by

surprise. "Is there something I can do to make it right?"

"Oh," he said, "it's not the way it sounds. But my trouble really began on the day you went into court with the Dragons."

I remember very clearly that time when I was so strangely guided to try to help those seven New York boys who killed Michael Farmer. I searched my memory, but I couldn't remember that this minister had had anything to do with the case.

He read my thoughts. "No," he said, "I wasn't there. I was hundreds of miles away. But I read in the newspapers about how you were thrown out of the Dragons' courtroom.

"Brother Wilkerson, when I saw your picture in the paper, something took hold of me. I said, 'That man is only there for publicity. They ought to take his ordination papers away from him.'

"I guess it was envy, pure and simple. But what a green-eyed dragon it has been in my life. I got so I would lie awake at night thinking evil thoughts about what you were doing. Everything I heard about your work made it worse. They tell me that I started denouncing you in my sermons, and in one of them I broke down completely.

"I lost my parish, Brother Wilkerson—all because I couldn't stand the thought of what you were accomplishing. Now, with God's help, I think I'm on the road to recovery. When I learned you were coming to this city, I decided to confess to your face my malicious feelings toward you all these years. I know now that I was only destroying myself, and I beg your forgiveness for all the evil I have thought and said."

Of course I had been completely unaware of all this, and I was ready and willing to forgive. I left that weeping minister, amazed at the amount of time he had been in torment. For the time since the newsmen's flash bulbs popped in my face at the trial of the seven Dragons had been *ten years*.

A New York schoolteacher was arrested for prostitution. This lady may have talked about high ideals by day, but by night she showed the morals of an alley cat. One of the youth organizations I admire is the Scouting program, but I know of one Scout leader who molested the young boys he was supposed to be guiding. When fifteen teen-agers were arrested in a western community for experimenting with marijuana, it was found that their supplier was a deacon in a local church. A woman in another community had pill parties for teen-agers.

No, I have to admit that we adults hardly set our young people an ideal example. Take the matter of drugs. In spite of the fast-increasing drug addiction among teen-agers, the fact is that adults may be the worst drug abusers of all. Thousands of seemingly successful middle-aged residents of quiet suburban communities are hooked on amphetamines and barbiturates. Some of them take cocktails to relax, then take pills to get over the hangover, then more pills for pep, then more cocktails to relax again—in a desperate cycle they can't stop.

Alcohol, by the way, is an addictive drug. It kills 20,000 Americans a year in highway accidents alone, and it is mixed up with nearly half the crimes in the country. No wonder many pot-smoking juveniles are disgusted with parents who are hooked on booze.

Tobacco is another addictive drug which millions of adults use legally. There is no question any more that cigarettes endanger health and life. Many people know that cigarette smokers have ten times the lung cancer death rate of non-smokers. But it is less widely realized that regular smokers have more of *every* disease, statistically, than their non-smoking neighbors—including more deaths from bronchitis, cancer of the esophagus, cancer of the bladder, cancer of the stomach, and heart disease. So the old description of cigarettes as coffin nails was exactly on target.

No wonder a good many hippies say that their parents are phonies who can't exist without their own fifths of whiskey and their cafeterias of pills—and all of whose advice is therefore worthless.

So I acknowledge a real measure of sympathy with the point of view of the young person who expressed his feelings about the older generation as follows:

"Look at you, blowing up whole countries for the sake of some crazy ideologies that you don't live up to anyway. Look at you, deceiving a whole generation of kids into getting a revolving charge account and buying your junk. (Who's a junkie?) Look at you, needing a couple of stiff drinks before you have the guts to talk with another human being. Look at you, making it with your neighbor's wife on the sly just to try and prove that you're really alive. Look at you, hooked on *your* cafeteria of pills, and making up dirty names for anybody who isn't in your bag, and messing up the land and the water and the air for profit, and calling this nowhere scene the Great Society! And you're gonna tell us how to live? C'mon, man, you've got to be kidding!" (*It's Happening*, J. L. Simmons and Barry Winograd).

There's a whole lot in what these kids say that I can't help buying. Whenever they rebel against phoniness and rottenness, I'm with them. I can't forget the Man who saw right through the respected leaders of His day. Those men were very good at making prayers, but Jesus knew that fundamentally they were about as straight as corkscrews. He told them:

"Impostors! You take advantage of widows and rob them of their homes, and then make a show of making long prayers! Because of this your punishment will be all the worse!

"Impostors! You give to God one tenth even of the seasoning herbs, such as mint, dill, and cummin, but you neglect to obey the really important teachings of the Law, such as justice and mercy and honesty . . . . Blind guides! You strain a fly out of your drink, but swallow a camel!

"Impostors! You clean the outside of your cup and plate, while the inside is full of things you have gotten by violence and selfishness . . . on the outside you appear to everybody as good, but inside you are full of lies and sins" (Matthew 23:14, 23-25,28, *Good News for Modern Man*).

I'm convinced that a lot of young people today would applaud if they heard anyone talk that way to the leaders of the establishment.

Of course there is a completely different side to the modern world; the phoniness and deception are so glaring partly because of their contrast with a whole lot that's fine and genuine. I have tremendous respect for the thousands of dedicated businessmen, legislators, ministers and missionaries and laymen who are truly "the salt of the earth."

And adults aren't the only phonies!

13

False Fronts

At the close of a crusade in one great city, dozens of teen-agers came forward to "come clean" with God. As the other workers and I moved among these young people, we heard them sobbing out some shocking stories of sin and guilt.

One boy had stolen a car, wrecked it, and thereby crippled one of the riders for life. Several boys and girls had been involved in sex parties with activities so sordid that I would never permit the details to be put into print. Others had experimented with marijuana and goof-balls, taken part in organized shoplifting, and nearly ruined their lives in many forms of youthful rebellion. All of them had heard God speaking to their hearts in the crusade, and now they were pouring out their confessions. As I saw the slim young shoulders of many of them shaking with grief, I realized what agonies they were experiencing. Yet at the same time I knew that these young people were ridding their lives and consciences of an evil past, and that the Great Physician was probing many a young life to heal and renew.

In the middle of all this, I noticed at one side of the auditorium a young man with horn-rimmed glasses

and two young women, one with a small notebook
and a pen in her hand. They looked as though they
might have just graduated from some university, and
at first I hoped that the three of them would come
forward to counsel some of the sobbing teen-agers. I
soon learned why they didn't.

All three came over to me, and the young woman
with the notebook, who seemed to be their spokes-
man, smiled brightly as she spoke. "We are students
at City Theological Seminary. We are studying the
phenomena of religious revivalism, and of course we
are deeply interested in the socio-economic factors in
urban delinquency. But we do not approve of the
emotionalism you are fostering here. Really, isn't
there a more rational approach to youth problems
than making all these adolescents weep and confess
their sins in public like this? Is all this emotionalism
necessary? We have watched you use crowd psychology and hypnotic suggestion to work these young
people into this frenzy, and we do not approve."

I like to think as I look back, that this young woman's remarks produced within me a healthy reaction
of purely righteous indignation. Certainly this was a
challenge I had no desire to duck. But I'll tell you the
truth: These three made me mad.

I backed all three of them up against the wall and
shook my finger in the face of the young lady with the
pen and the notebook, and I barely tried to control
my anger as I answered her.

"I'm surprised that students from a theological seminary are able to see what you have seen and talk the
way you do. You don't recognize the working of God
when you see it. I think all three of you are in a very

dangerous condition—I believe you once knew God, and you too knew what it was like long ago to love lost souls, but you have left that first love. Your hearts have grown death-cold, and you are in danger of committing the unpardonable sin."

I saw the young man turn a trifle pale, but I continued. "You think you have all the answers, but you haven't offered me one practical suggestion for reaching human need. Look at these kids! Some of the boys have been stealing automobiles, some of the girls are pregnant, some of them are on pills—and all of them are sick inside. They need help. Yet you have the gall to stand there and tell me that I have no right to let these youngsters show some emotion as they confess their sins to God and seek His healing power! What you need is to get on your knees like these kids, and cry to God for help as earnestly as they are."

Both young women opened their mouths and began to reply, but then a strange thing happened. Their faces started to crumple, at almost the same moment, and to my amazement all three of these students suddenly fell to their knees and began to sob.

I watched God work. One by one the students confessed that they had lost their faith and let a cold spirit of critical pride take its place. The three had been making it a habit to attend meetings like mine, pick the preacher apart, corner him after the service, and then try to set him straight!

As I flew away from that city I thanked God that those three young people would not become church leaders with more theory than faith. This experience, I was sure, would help them lead a good many men

and women and young people into a real relationship
with Jesus Christ.

The three students, I reflected, had been hiding behind a false front—one of spiritual pride and unbelief.
A lot of young people hide behind false fronts.

One of them is the Confusion Front. I know many
of the youngsters who put up this particular front.
Their attitude is summed up in the words of a young
hippie who wandered into our Teen Challenge coffee-
shop, The Lost Coin, and smirkingly said to our workers, "I don't dig this business of what God expects of
me. And I don't understand the Bible at all; it just
doesn't make sense."

In crusades I have held in cities all over the world,
young people have said to me, "How can I turn my
life over to Christ? I don't get it. I guess I'm just
mixed up."

If you could fit that picture, I'm going to tell you
something you won't like. I think it is absolutely dis-
honest to hide behind a front of ignorance or confusion. It is inconceivable to me that young people who
have learned how to do equations in algebra, to understand the basic facts of modern psychology and
science, or to get a job or a driver's license, cannot understand something as simple as the gospel of Christ.
The gospel is not nearly as complicated as the new
math, yet intelligent young people claim they can't
dig it.

I've heard young hippies with Gandhi spectacles
and sandals, who probably make straight A's in
school, claim they can't understand Jesus' gospel, or
say the Bible is irrelevant. In the cafes of Greenwich
Village or Haight-Ashbury they discuss these things

with an air of superiority and finality, but the fact is that *most of them have never really investigated the claims or evidences of Christianity*. Why? Surely many of them don't lack intellectual "candle power." Are they too lazy to fight the modern tide of doubt and disbelief? Here's one area where I wish these nonconformists would refuse to conform!

But it seems "hip" today to disbelieve almost everything that has been believed in the past. It is popular to call this flat unbelief "intellectual investigation." But it is really defiance of facts and logic.

The basic question is whether there is a Power greater than ourselves, whether there is a God who made us and has the right to guide our lives, or not. Common sense says that we didn't make ourselves. And if you admit the common sense logic of God, you can't evade Him long by playing one religion or one argument against another. Sure, there are questions some of us may not be able to answer completely, but that figures; a God we could understand completely wouldn't be a very big God. The important issue is the fact of God.

Christianity rests on one mighty important fact: God communicates His love and power clearly to us, through the Bible, through Jesus Christ and through the Holy Spirit. We don't need to grope around in the dark looking for God. He is the One who is looking for us, and He sent Jesus to earth to prove it. God wants us all in His eternal family.

Time after time I have seen young people quit the confused act, get on their knees, and really let the Lord into their hearts. That's the important thing. Jesus is saying today, "Behold, I stand at the door, and knock" (Revelation 3:20). With Him, everything begins to straighten out. This process may take time, but accepting Jesus Christ is the beginning.

Then there's the phony Religion Front. That false front sometimes exists even in genuine Christian churches. I'm guessing that you know the kind of person I mean. He or she talks big about faith and prayer —in front of Christian friends—but has a completely different line, and life, with others. He's one person in church, and a completely different person in school or on the streets.

The churches today are filled with "goodniks"— young persons who grew up in church and know all the right religious phrases, who have been taught all there is to learn about the basic teachings of Christianity, who go to all the church functions, but who do not know Christ Himself. They have had more opportunity than other young people to accept Him, but they have never made that crucial decision.

Some of these goodniks, I suspect, are good only because they're too lazy to be bad. They may not steal, but they will cheat in school. They do not swear, but they stretch the truth clear out of shape. They would never have premarital intercourse, but they break the seventh commandment in spirit.

There's even a phony Repentance Front.

Tony was twenty years old when he came to Teen Challenge for help. In my office, he put his head on my desk and sobbed like a baby as he told his story:

"Mr. Wilkerson, drugs have ruined my life. Because of them I've lost my wife and my two children—I'm the most desperate, needy guy in New York. Please take me in, give me a bed, help me regain my health and be a good man. I want to be good; I want to be clean. Please help me, Mr. Wilkerson; please, please help me be better!"

Tony went on and on, and the more he talked, the more sure I was that he was putting on an act. There are drug addicts who will commit a crime and deliberately get themselves jailed for a strange reason: Normally, in prison they cannot get drugs, and they lose their physical dependence on them. Then when they "shoot it up" again as soon as they get out of prison, they recapture the thrill they experienced the first time they tried it, as the heroin shoots into their now near-normal veins. Also, the habit costs less until their drug tolerance expands again.

Convinced that this was Tony's real motive in coming to me, I interrupted his spiel. I looked him straight in the eye and said coldly, "I think you are a phony. I've helped a good many addicts, and I can tell when someone is just crying crocodile tears. I think you love that junk you've been shooting into your veins, and you don't want to kick your habit at all.

"Get out on the street," I said; "really get desperate, and then come to me when you mean what you say. I can smell it all over you—*you're a phony.*"

I don't suppose Tony ever expected a religious worker to talk to him like that. He looked as stunned as if I had stabbed him, and he pleaded with me to take him in.

I was not convinced. I asked him to leave.

About ten minutes later, however, there was a knock on my door. It was Glen, one of our Teen Challenge staff workers. "Mr. Wilkerson, please come to the front door of the Center."

There Glen pointed down the street. Halfway down the block was Tony, on his knees with his arms around a tree, sobbing his heart out.

"Glen," I said, "that's a good act, but it's only an act." I could see Glen was going to have to learn a lesson the hard way, so I added, "All right, you go get him, bring him back and give him a bed—in your room. You've got to help him kick it cold turkey."

As you probably know, at Teen Challenge, when an addict stops taking drugs he has to do it "cold turkey." We don't believe in a long-drawn-out withdrawal period. We make each addict stop taking drugs at once, and the painful withdrawal from dependence on a powerful drug is called cold turkey. The name may come from the fact that in that agonizing process the addict's skin often breaks out in gooseflesh, like a turkey's rough skin.

Glen ran down the street, talked to Tony, and invited him back to the Center. He pumped my hand with seemingly overwhelming gratitude: "Mr. Wilkerson, you'll never be sorry. I'll make it if anybody makes it. I'm really desperate. I need help."

I just silently nodded my head, and I whispered to myself, *We'll see.*

For the next two and a half days, Tony never missed a meal. He was always first in the chow line—but the last person to enter chapel. During the daily services, he bowed his head in prayer and took part in the singing when he noticed me watching him, but the rest of the time he yawned and was obviously completely bored.

I knew what would happen the third day Tony was with us, and sure enough, it did. A number of young addicts testified that day how Christ had changed their lives and cured them of the desire for drugs. As they talked, Tony grew more and more restless. When we stood to sing a hymn, Tony got to his feet and went out the door. One of the staff members saw him running down the street like a jackrabbit—straight for the subway.

Ten minutes later Glen was in my office. "Now I know what you mean," he said abashedly. "Tony wasn't ready for help—he was just putting on a big front. Maybe I'll know better next time."

We get quite a few of these phony Christian Fronters at Teen Challenge, especially when they first arrive. Some of them kneel at the altar and tell us they're changed, but the change is only in their talk. They sneak away for a puff of marijuana or a shot of dope whenever they get a chance. But they find that they can't have it both ways. Eventually they have to make a choice: all the way with Jesus, or back to the hell of the gutter and the dead-end life. Thank God, hundreds of them choose Him.

I have often wondered why more and more young people are trying beer, wine, and every mind-twisting drug that is invented. Why are so many turning to dirty literature and illegitimate sex? Why do young men aim their hot rods at each other and flirt with death on the highways? High school hops are crowded with kids losing themselves in the beat of drums and the twanging of guitars, letting themselves go.

This Go-Go age is described by the prophet Isaiah: "They snatch on the right hand and are still hungry,

and eat on the left hand and are not satisfied" (9:20).
Young people are ready to try anything, and are willing to follow the crowd right to hell, but they are not
satisfied. They are calling: "Fulfill my longings. Meet
my needs. Fill the emptiness in my heart. Set me free
from my terrible cravings."

But those cravings only grow into more and more
diabolical demands unless the heart itself is satisfied
with what it needs most of all. A wise man named
Augustine who lived fifteen hundred years ago once
said, "Thou hast made us for Thyself, and our hearts
are restless until they rest in Thee."

That is still true.

When Christ comes into a life, all the cravings for
things that cannot satisfy begin to go. All the false
fronts begin tumbling down, and you begin to experience the wonderful relief of being on the level, at last,
with everyone.

To every young person who is searching for truth
and reality, I wish I could say this: "You *can* be real
in a phony age. God gave you a good mind; use it to
find the truth and to expose some of the frauds that
are all around the landscape. Don't buy all the propaganda that's being handed out these days. Be genuine, be your *best* self, and don't be afraid to be completely different from the phonies!"

14

Learning to Be Ordinary

I suspect that most people start wearing these false fronts I've been talking about for the same reason that so many of the drug addicts I meet took to narcotics —because they felt they were failures. In our age it is an unforgivable sin to fail. Getting high—and wearing a false front—gives people a fleeting sense of achievement, even though it finally produces some *real* failures.

And one of the biggest problems ahead of most young people is non-success. Most of the young people growing up today will never be television idols, will never have their pictures in the sports pages of the newspapers, will never produce smash hits on Broadway, will never write best-sellers, will never be corporation executives, and will never turn the world upside down.

Unless you believe the ads and commercials. All you need for popularity and success, we are constantly told by the advertisers, is to use the right deodorant, pick the right perfume, smoke the right cigarette, buy the right toothpaste, use the right hair conditioner, or rinse with the right mouthwash. If you can't sleep, there is no problem—just take Comfee-

Snooz. Tired, run down, ache all over? Don't worry, we've got a little pill for that. Eat or drink too much? Just take two doses of Hangover Blitz and you're a new man or woman. Been yelling too much at people? Then all you need is a tablet of Soothe.

It's not funny. Young people are led to believe that if they take the right courses, meet the right people, memorize the right formulas, smell good, and smile with gleaming teeth, brilliant successes will drop right into their laps. Our whole way of life is a pressure cooker in which ordinary youngsters are turned into neurotic, maladjusted, success-seeking, miserable, aspirin-popping adults.

It begins early. The first time little Tommy hits a home run in Little League, someone starts grooming him for the big leagues. When Susan gets a solo part in choir, she's told she is another Doris Day. The children's teachers keep telling them that every year in school is worth so many more dollars of income. The libraries overflow with books on how to take ten easy steps to the top, how to get power over others with the right mental gimmicks, and how to make millions without trying.

Even religion has been infiltrated by the success cult. Churches and religious organizations prove that God is blessing them by pointing to the number of members on the roll or the number of dollars in the till. Some religious people seem to be trying to tell us: "Last year I only made $50,000, but this year I obeyed the Lord and made my first million."

Of course God is not against the comforts of life—if they are held lightly. He gives every good and perfect gift. But prosperity and success are ours for only one reason—to use in His work. The poverty of Jesus Christ, and the tremendous struggles and frustrations of millions of His saints, illustrate the fact that what we know as success may have nothing to do with real religion.

Many young people are fed up with the emptiness and phoniness of a money-centered culture. A great many of them want more out of life than big cars, homes on half-acre lots, swimming pools and mink. They want to join the cause of someone more concerned with sharing than with shaving. So some of them quit their jobs, take off their shoes, let their hair grow, wear sloppy clothes, stop bathing, and burn dollar bills in protest against paper money and plastic values.

I'm not justifying the hippies. To me burning money looks just as idiotic as it must to you, and I agree that what many of the hippies need is a good shaking and a trip to the barber. I'm not knocking the capitalistic system which can provide so many worthwhile products for so many millions of people. I'm not pleading for either dropouts or cop-outs, and I'm not downgrading success.

I *am* calling for a philosophy of life by which young people can accept being ordinary—in other words, accept the fact that they are only human. Most of us are superior in some way to certain people we know and inferior to others. We have to learn to live with that fact. And we need to be able to face our limitations, and to live with such things as loneliness and failure.

We also need to learn that we don't have to claw our way to the top of the heap. The majority who will never make it there anyway can save themselves a lot of anxiety and wear and tear if they learn to be content with themselves as they are—and if they learn to live with their *real* needs.

A person's real needs are very simple. He must learn to live with himself, with other people, and with God. I like to think of this as a triangle with equal sides. One side represents self, one side others, and one side God. If one side is out of proportion, all of life can get maladjusted.

Most of us have known people who seemed very dedicated to God, but who couldn't live with their neighbors. Some well-meaning individuals can't stand people. I had to let one very promising young man leave our Teen Challenge staff becuase he had never learned to get along with himself.

Let's start with that side of the triangle. *Everyone must learn to live with himself.* Some of the most miserable people on earth have never learned to do this. They love God, they are nice to others, but they hate themselves. Their favorite feeling may be, "I'm no good."

I have met many people who seem to have convinced themselves that they will never live up to what God expects of them. They fear they will barely get to heaven—if they get there at all. They seem to think, "I'm just a failure—I've tried, but I keep stumbling; I guess it's just my lot to be the way I am."

Sometimes such an attitude covers up a serious situation. Many people who say "I'm no good" are trying to confess: "There is a secret sin in my life which I cannot conquer. I've certainly tried hard enough; it must be that I'm no good."

To such people I say: *Stop belittling yourself.* There is no virtue in that. Moses kept telling God that he was unworthy of the task he had been given, and God asked. "What is that in your hand?"

"A rod."

"Drop it," said God. That probably didn't make sense to Moses; the rod must have seemed harmless enough. But as he dropped it, the rod became a serpent. There may be something you love that God wants you to drop. If so, drop it; it may seem harmless enough, but there may be a serpent in it.

Then God challenged, "Pick it up." Have you ever tried to pick up a snake? God wants us to go after all the snakes in our lives. Get hold of them, and believe that God can transform each one into a rod of power and victory—as He did for Moses.

Take an inventory of your life. Analyze yourself; learn to recognize both your abilities and your limitations, your successes and your failures. You may have failed to achieve some wonderful goal you set for yourself long ago. But this is no reason to follow the failure trail all through life. Get back on your feet! And this time set reasonable goals.

When I see a hippie artist painting on a street corner, I look for some talent in him. Usually it's a hopeless task; most of these would-be artists have not sold five dollars' worth of paintings and never will. Their whole rebellion is often the result of failing to achieve something they set out to reach. They would achieve much more if they would admit, "I'm not an artist; I'm just doing this as a hobby." Then they might find a satisfactory life if they would just learn to be ordinary.

We must also learn to live with other people. The average person has not learned such an ordinary thing as to live at peace with his fellow men. All over the globe, husbands are fighting with their wives, employers with their workers, whites with colored people, the haves with the have-nots. And there will be no real peace on earth until many more of us learn to get along with the other human beings on our planet.

Here is a secret that works wonders in helping people get along together better. Try this test. Write the name of the person you have been having trouble with at the top of a sheet of paper. List at least three good things about that person. Now, on a second sheet, write your own name—and list about fifty of your faults. (If you're honest, I don't think this will take too long. It wouldn't for me!) Then compare the two lists—and thank God for His blessing in that other person's life.

Learn to rejoice in the good in others. Walk away from all group discussions that turn into character assassination. Never form an opinion about someone on the basis of gossip or hearsay. Believe the best of others in spite of all you hear.

One of the great evangelists of our day practices this continually. Some may think he is too trusting, but he doesn't get ulcers over alleged faults in other Christians. Instead, he looks on the best side of everyone he knows. An associate of his told a friend of mine, "In spite of all the criticisms that have been made of him, never once have I heard him say anything critical or unkind about his critics."

Once when my wife, Gwen, was hospitalized, someone at a church gathering called for prayer "because of the trouble Reverend Wilkerson is having with his wife." A man was there who had held a grudge against me for years. Without waiting to find out what our "trouble" was, this man rushed out to spread the rumor far and near: "Mr. Wilkerson is leaving his wife." Miraculously, the rumor was killed. But it never would have started if someone hadn't been looking for evil, and if he hadn't been eager to spread a false report without investigating the facts.

It's important to learn how to live with yourself, and with other people. But the most important thing anyone can ever do is to learn to live with God—to know Him, and to do what He wants.

Young person, God wants you to listen to three things. He pleads, *"Talk to Me."* He wants you to pour out your deepest thoughts and hopes and fears to Him. Just talk to Him simply; tell Him all about everything that is on your mind and heart. Peace with God depends on learning to do this.

Many times I have been so blue, or lonely, or upset or sad and empty that I felt almost hopeless. But after a time in the secret presence of God, I have come away lifted, happy and blessed.

God also begs you, *"Trust My love for you."* He is Love, He loves us in our weakness and failure, and He will love us forever. The biggest mistake you can ever make is to think, "God will not forgive me." This is to deny His love and Christ's work. We spend so much time trying to measure our love for God when we really ought to be trying to measure His love for us. Read about this in Ephesians 3:18-19.

Also, God commands, *"Stop fretting and fussing."* Sometimes we get very restless and unhappy waiting

for God to do something. We may get the idea that
He is too busy or too big (or not big enough?) to take
care of *us*. And we make a lot of trouble for ourselves
by taking things into our own hands and then messing
everything up.

A while ago I told my little son Gary about a trip
our family was going to take to visit a friend in Ohio.
I got out some road maps and explained the route,
and Gwen told Gary about the Ohio cousins and aunt
and uncle we hadn't seen for some time.

Gary got so excited about the trip that it seemed he
was asking, "How soon do we start?" every fifteen
minutes for two weeks. Then the trip began. Twenty
minutes later Gary asked, "How soon do we get
there?" And all through the trip he and his brother
Greg kept asking, "Are we there yet, Daddy? How
much farther? Won't we ever get there, Daddy?"

And I realized that our heavenly Father has a lot of
grownup children who act just like those boys. We
can't wait for God to do something, and as soon as He
begins, we can't wait until He has finished. And sometimes we must try His patience with our restlessness
and lack of faith.

Talk to God much—but fill your heart with His limit-
less love, and learn to trust Him all the way.

Jack Kerouac, who gave the word "beat" a new
meaning a few years ago, was once asked an important question by an interviewer: "This 'beat' generation
has been described as a seeking generation. What are
you looking for?"

"God," answered Jack Kerouac. "I want God to
show me His face."

Sometimes it looks as though this generation is

spending all its energies trying to get rid of God, but at the same time it's surprising how much the anti-God protesters talk about God and religion. One of Bob Dylan's most popular songs is "Outside the Gates of Eden," people crowd into motion picture theaters to see Bible epics, and young people taking LSD together cry, "Let's all be Jesus." The hippies eat "soul food" and campaign for love, peace, and hope.

A lot of this religion is irreverent nonsense, but still I think it is true that what young people are searching for today is basically a spiritual experience. The church has failed to show them the way. Yet none of them will be truly satisfied until they find God.

15

The Flower People . . .
and the Future

Everywhere I went as I traveled through Europe last fall I was surprised by the number of hippies I met. From Paris and Berlin to Copenhagen and Stockholm, I saw droves of teen-agers who looked as though they had just flown in from Greenwich Village or Haight-Ashbury. They went barefoot or wore sandals and old jeans and miniskirts topped with loose shirts and sweaters. Bells tinkled as they moved. Both sexes tended to wear their hair as long as possible—just like in America. And they carried flowers.

As I mentioned earlier, these turned-on European youngsters don't like to be known as beatniks or hippies. They insist on being called the Flower People. One nineteen-year-old boy told me very seriously, "I love the flowers and the trees. After I die I will return as a bird, and then I can enjoy the world more than ever."

Like their counterparts elsewhere, the Flower People put a lot of emphasis on love. They usually travel in groups, live together, oppose all forms of violence, and share what they have very generously. They remind me a lot of the groups I come across frequently in Greenwich Village.

The Village is filled with little communities with strange ideals. One of these is the Kerista group, whose motto is "Love Conquers All." The members dream of migrating to an island in the Caribbean where they can live in peace and harmony and can rear their children in their new way of life.

Kerista began when a businessman felt that he had a divine revelation. A chorus of voices told him that Kerista was to be the new religion of the world. This was the burden of their message:

> *The hatred and strife which divide man from man must speedily come to an end. Humanity's age-long aspirations for peace and perfection are about to be actualized. Every individual must be granted complete and total freedom, that the personal development of every child of God may reach its zenith. Through Kerista will come about a higher evolutionary consciousness for all, and the dreams of the ages will be accomplished.*

Another religious group that seems to be growing in popularity in the Village these days is made up of Krishna worshipers. You may have seen them if you've ever gone through Tompkins Square Park on a Sunday afternoon. The members sit cross-legged on a blanket while one or two of their group slowly circle in a dance. To the beat of bongo drums and the ringing of bells, the worshipers—who could pass for college students but for their garb—sing over and over:

> *Hare Krishna, Hare Krishna,*
> *Krishna, Krishna! Hare, Hare.*

> *Hare Rama, Hare Rama,*
> *Rama, Rama! Hare, Hare.*

The young men, heads shaved except for a lock at the back of the head, favor yellow T-shirts and flowing saffron-colored trousers. The young women go in for loose robes and long hair. All of them have white streaks of paint down their foreheads, bare feet, and strings of beads and owl-eyed idols around their necks. A pot of incense burns nearby as the worshipers continue to dance and sing hypnotically, over and over. The chant rings out, mingling with the sound of bells from the steeples of the neighborhood's old churches: *Hare Krishna, Hare Krishna. . . .*

Krishna and Rama are two of the incarnations of the Hindu god Vishnu; Krishna is the god of amorous love and Rama is one of Hinduism's many saviors. The Krishna worshipers often hold street meetings in Greenwich Village, ringing their bells, singing their song, and handing out literature.

The Village scene is constantly changing. Today there is a trend toward action and group activity. Do-it-yourself art shops and Happenings are frequent. Some of the activities are constructive and disarming. Recently Third Street had a sweep-in. The hippies soaped the streets, cleaned basements, cleared vacant lots, and painted the fire hydrants and sewer tops silver and gold. And they gave away bananas.

Last May Orky and his buddies brought pails of paint and brushes to the police station on Fifth Street and offered to paint the dingy walls, but their generous gesture was rebuffed and they were thrown out. Later they offered to wash the police cars, but the police were unenthusiastic.

The big theme of the hippies is love. After the Third Street sweep-in these words were left painted on the walls of buildings: *Because We Love*. A year ago on Easter Sunday the hippies had a be-in at Central Park. Shouting *"Love!"* they pelted the police with daffodils. The cops didn't know how to react! A cartoonist memorialized the event with a drawing of a policeman phoning headquarters: "They are attacking now with gladiolas and chrysanthemums."

In their search for love, though, the hippies and the Flower People have a long way to go. Their idea of love is shallow and selfish in comparison to the love God has shown in giving us His Son. When the Flower People meet Jesus Christ, they find out how strong and wonderful love really is. They discover that *real* love works miracles.

While I was in Darmstadt, Germany, last fall, I spoke to more than two thousand people of all ages in a church known as the Jesus House. This is an amazing place built by Mother Basilia Schlink, who heads an order of Protestant nuns dedicated to reconciliation among men and with God. Mother Schlink had put placards everywhere announcing, "DAVID IS COMING."

The Flower People came by the busloads. When the Jesus House ran out of seats, these European hippies sprawled on the floor, and some of them began cursing and smoking. I made them behave. Then I gave the same kind of message I preached throughout Europe.

I read these words from the ancient prophet Joel:

Let the priests, the ministers of the Lord, weep between the porch and the altar, and let them say, Spare thy people, O Lord, and give not thine heritage to reproach, that the heathen should rule over them: wherefore should they say among the people, Where is their God? Then will the Lord be jealous for his land, and pity his people . . . .

And it shall come to pass afterward, that I will pour out my Spirit upon all flesh; and your sons and your daughters shall prophesy, your old men shall dream dreams, your young men shall see visions: And also upon the servants and upon the handmaids in those days will I pour out my Spirit" (Joel 2:17-18, 28-29).

When I extended the invitation that night, more than three hundred Flower People responded. Twenty clergymen came to me to ask for prayer, and I laid my hands on their heads as I prayed, asking God to transmit His power through them to others. One of the men was a priest who said, "Reverend Brother David, I am going back to my altar to pray until I find more of this power which has been demonstrated in our midst."

Here is the new kind of ecumenism God is bringing to pass—not based on expanding the ecclesiastical machinery or patching up the outward differences, but built on the power of the Holy Spirit in reaching a lost generation.

While I was going through Europe I had a memorable visit to Brussels, where the new trade center for the Common Market is being built. The administrative headquarters of the European Economic Community, Brussels is fast becoming the commercial capital of Europe and the economic hub of the world. A fine modern city, Brussels has attracted businessmen and their families from many countries, including America.

I had lunch with the pastor of a great Brussels church. He startled me by saying, "I do not believe in your concept of winning souls to Christ, or of being born again. I can't imagine anyone's life actually being changed."

"Tell me something," I said. "How do *you* help young people? When the servicemen, the drug addicts, and the teen-agers who are in trouble come to you, what do you do?"

"Frankly," he said, "I don't do anything. If anyone came to me asking for help, I'd be scared to death."

When I preached in Brussels that night, this minister was in the congregation along with many of the young people of his church. I made a simple presentation of the gospel and I predicted that a spiritual awakening was beginning.

When I gave the invitation to find Christ, dozens of young people responded—and the first to come were members of the church whose pastor did not believe in changed lives. My heart tugged with sympathy toward those Brussels young people as they talked about their lives. They told me of their long hikes on foot and by bike, of their private Swiss schools and their parents' social activities, of sex involvement. They said that in spite of all this, life did not seem worth living; they felt empty and dead. They also said something like this: "This is the first time we ever met Jesus Christ. Now we know what you mean when you talk about that spiritual awakening."

The next revolution is on the way. I predict that we are on the brink of the greatest spiritual renewal in history. Young people everywhere in the world are about to witness the power of the Holy Spirit in action. Get ready, get set—God's time has come!

If you wish to share in the
Reverend David Wilkerson's
work, his address is:

Teen Challenge, Inc.
444 Clinton Avenue
Brooklyn, New York 11238